Cynthia

Hope you enjoy
the book

love
Norma 1988

Barmy

Victoria Wood

BARMY
The New Victoria Wood Sketch Book
Featuring 'Acorn Antiques'

METHUEN · LONDON

by the same author

Lucky Bag: The Victoria Wood Song Book
Up to You, Porky: The Victoria Wood Sketch Book

First published in Great Britain in 1987
by Methuen London Ltd
11 New Fetter Lane, London EC4P 4EE
Reprinted 1987 (twice)
Copyright © Victoria Wood 1987
Made and printed in Great Britain
by R. Clay Ltd, Chichester, Sussex
Photoset by Rowland Phototypesetting Ltd
Bury St Edmunds, Suffolk

British Library Cataloguing in Publication Data

Wood, Victoria
    Barmy: the new Victoria Wood sketch book.
    I. Title
    828'.91409   PN6175

    ISBN 0-413-16870-0

To Susie, Ceal, Duncan, and Julie
– for the acting

Contents

List of Illustrations

Preface

Joan   And now it's over to Margery, who's been looking at what's out on the bookstalls this week for those of us who enjoy a jolly good read. *(Strolls over.)* Hello Margery, what's out on the bookstalls this week for those of us who enjoy a jolly good read?

Margery   Hello Joan. Well there's a bumper crop of goodies available, and a varied assortment they are too.

Joan   Golly. For instance.

Margery   *Glamour*, a powerful family saga of a Salford mill girl's rise from the depression-hit thirties to the heights of Hollywood. There's *Saga*, a family story of height-hitting Hollywood glamour and power in the depression, and *Salford*, that's just very depressing.

Joan   And are they full of liberated thirty-five-year-old women doing unspeakably erotic things to bronzed muscly tycoons?

Margery   Yes they are Joan, so to save a lot of tedious explanations I've brought you a book on tapestry.

Joan   Of course not everything in the publishing world is fiction, is it Margery? There's non-fiction for instance.

Margery   That's right Joan. Investigative journalist Campbell Wemyss has brought out *Crippen – Was It Pre-Menstrual Tension?*, and *Country Diary of an Edwardian Lady* lovers will be delighted to hear that there will be a new cake tin out next month.

Joan   And finally and very quickly Margery, comedy.

Margery   Finally and very quickly Joan, the funniest book for years fell into my lap this morning. Devastatingly outspoken, a real rib-tickler but with plenty of pathos as well, it really deserves a much wider audience.

Joan   And that's Victoria Wood's second book of sketches, is it, Margery?

Margery   No, it's your diary Joan, you left it on the incinerator in the second floor Ladies. Bye!

Joan   Bye!

Barmy

Nora

Nora	Hello. Have you ever planted your bulbs out in the Autumn and watched them come up in the Spring? Have you? Lovely, arent' they?

Have you ever been out in the garden just after an April shower, and mmm, breathed in that wonderful fresh smell? It's the grass and the leaves saying thank you, really, isn't it?

And have you ever been up on a step-ladder and lost your balance, and grabbed at a frayed light fitting with your bare hand, and been electrocuted? I have. Ooh, it didn't half sting.

And have you ever tried to lose weight by having your jaws wired together, and found you were up half the night trying to liquidize peanut brittle? My neighbour has.

Because life's not fair, is it? Some of us drink champagne in the fast lane, and some of us eat our sandwiches by the loose chippings on the A597.

Ooh – and it makes me mad when people complain – I mean if it starts to rain what do you do? Stick a brolly up.

And do you know what I'd like to do to these moaners and miserable complainers – stick a brolly up! I would.

No Gossip

Tea shop. Two nice ladies

First lady   Did you go to see 'Macbeth'?

Second lady   Mmmm. Wasn't a patch on 'Brigadoon'. There was some terrible woman who kept washing her hands, saying she'd never get them clean. I felt like shouting out 'Try Swarfega'. We walked out in the end.

First lady   Why?

Second lady   Someone said 'womb'.

First lady   No.

Second lady   Is said to Col – get your duffle – two pounds on a box of Quality Street and someone says womb.

First lady   It's happening all over.

Second lady   Oh I know. In my magazine story last week, an unmarried couple slept together.

First lady   Tuh.

Second lady   I mean, in my day, in a magazine, you didn't have sex, you had a row of dots.

First lady   That's right, three dots.

Second lady   In fact, still if Colin turns to me in the night, I just tap him three times on the shoulder and he goes to sleep quite happily.

First lady   Dot, dot, dot, yes.

Second lady   Except of course the children grew up thinking anything in Braille was pornographic.

First lady   How are the children?

Second lady   Well, Susan's still Assistant Catering Manager at Wilkinsons, and she says, in a couple of years, if she plays her cards right – she could become er, a catering manager's girlfriend.

First lady   Oh, that's good.

Second lady   And of course she's saving up for her bottom drawer.

First lady   Oh, what's she got?

Second lady	Just the knobs so far, but – oh, and she failed her test again.
First lady	Oh, what on?
Second lady	Something and nothing. Not looking in the mirror, and failing to report a couple of accidents.
First lady	And is Tony still in the SAS?
Second lady	No, he left.
First lady	I think you do have to be incredibly tough to stick it; the violence . . .
Second lady	And then you see, the balaclava was so itchy. And now he's a lighthouse keeper.
First lady	Goodness, that must be a lonely life – doesn't it affect him mentally?
Second lady	No, he keeps busy, grows a lot of vegetables. And he's fallen in love with a tomato.
First lady	An English tomato?
Second lady	Oh yes. He's sent us polaroids, she looks quite nice, still a bit green – but –
First lady	Has he got over his divorce?
Second lady	I think so. His wife got custody of the stereo and they sold the children.
First lady	And do you ever see your daughter-in-law?
Second lady	I do, funnily enough – she's our window cleaner.
First lady	That's women's lib for you.
Second lady	No, she's under a man. He's the skilled half, she just dunks the chammy. Anyway what about you?
First lady	Oh me? Same as ever.
Second lady	Still on that diet?
First lady	Still on my diet, still married to Ken, and still General Secretary of the United Nations.
Second lady	No gossip then.
First lady	No . . .

Margery and Joan: One

Joan	*(standing by a locked tank of water with a padlocked milk churn inside)* Well, your two minutes is up, Mr Jefferson, and I think we're going to have to leave it there for the time being. We'll possibly pop back a little later and see if Mr Jefferson did in fact manage to extricate himself from that milk churn. Now it's over to Margery to see what she's been getting up to this week. Hello, Margery – how's tricks?
Margery	Tricks? What do you mean?
Joan	I meant how are things going generally, Margery.
Margery	Oh, I thought Trix must be another of your god-awful friends in the Hush Puppies. *(Switching on the studio charm)* Hello, Joan. Now we all know about the frightening side-effects of barbiturate abuse, alcohol dependency and nicotine intake – but have you ever stopped to wonder about the dangers associated with these?

Shakes her closed fist à la nescafé, and opens her palm to the camera.

Joan	Now correct me if I'm wrong, Margery, but you've got a handful of ordinary industrial ball bearings.
Margery	Well you are wrong Joan, and I will correct you. Because what I'm holding is the contents of a standard fifty-gram packet of edible cake decorations.
Joan	Well I know that being hit over the head with an adjustable piano stool can give you a jolly nasty headache – but what's so dangerous about these little things, Margery?
Margery	The danger lies in the shiny metallic coating, Joan – the very sparkle that makes these little bimbos an indispensable part of every festivity and celebration from Christmas Day to Boxing Day.
Joan	And is the coating harmful, Margery?
Margery	No it's not, Joan. *(Picking up one ball)* But were a ball to come

into contact with a filling *(pointing one out)*, which can easily happen in a party situation . . .

Joan Someone showing off . . .

Margery Taking big bites to impress a girl; chewing with their mouth open –

Joan I must admit I've done that.

Margery Yes. The ball *(demonstrating)* makes contact with the filling and yaroo, an electric shock. Now one mild low-grade tingler every so often won't do too much damage – but if you've got a mouth full of fillings *and* a heavy cake eating habit – the sort of person who finds it difficult to refuse cake, or who needs cake to feel relaxed in a social situation – even the kind of compulsive chomper who doesn't eat it in public but takes a piece home wrapped in a serviette – then you could be at risk.

Joan And how can we minimize that risk, Margery?

Margery Just by taking a few simple precautions, Joan. *(Camera pulls back to show her feet encased in huge Wellingtons.)* Rubber footwear *(puts gloves on)*, insulated gloves, keep a fire blanket and portable resuscitator by the cake tin, have the phone number of your next of kin tattooed on an accessible part of your body – and – *(picking up cake and taking huge bite)* Happy Eating.

Music. Fade lights.

Joan I never went back to the man in the milk churn.

Faint sound of ambulance siren.

Margery *(mouth full of cake)* Too late now.

They look round vaguely.

Men Talking

Men in close-up, talking in their own homes.

First man *(sixties)* It was when I was at Freemans, I'd just started on the shop floor, and I was in the washroom, because you couldn't smoke on the floor, that's right – and my pal Eric said, 'Hey, Monkey' – this is before I was bald – 'Monkey – do you know anything about sex?' I said, 'No, I don't, do you?' And Eric said he didn't, but his brother knew. And his brother was on HMS Hastings, went down in forty-four, no survivors, so we never found out anything about it. Mind you – I suppose if I had got going with sex, I'd never have had this terrific involvement with miniature dynamos . . .

Second man *(forties)* And the children were in bed, and June and I were watching the television – it was a nature thing, something about dangerous butterflies – and June turned the volume down and said, 'I'm having an affair.' Silence. Then I said, 'Who with?' She said, 'You don't know him, he's a carpet salesman.' I said, 'Oh.' She said, 'I've told him he can move in on Tuesday, and can we move the hatstand so he's got somewhere to stack his underlay? Oh, and his name's Rory.' Which it was . . .

Third man *(thirties)* And she got more and more depressed. So I said, 'Look Sheila, if you're that desperate, go back to work and I'll stay at home and look after the baby.' So off she went. And I changed nappies, made the breakfast, did the hoovering, cleaned the cooker, made the beds, went shopping, fed the baby – and by lunchtime I'd had enough. I phoned Sheila at work – I said, 'You'll have to pack your job in, I can't stand it.' It's true.

Today in Hospital

Film. Morning. The front steps of a small hospital. A man is mopping the steps.

Corin   *(Voice Over)* It's seven-thirty in the morning. For some people this will just be an ordinary day, but for others accident or illness will mean they end up spending today in hospital.

TITLE 'TODAY IN HOSPITAL'

Corin hurries up the steps to the cleaner.

Corin   Good morning.
Cleaner   I don't mop steps as a hobby, you know.
Corin   How long have you worked at the hospital?
Cleaner   *(turning away)* They want to bring back National Service, in my opinion.

Corin goes into the hospital.

Casualty. Small and empty except for a young couple, Elaine and Conrad. Corin goes over to the receptionist.

Corin   Is Casualty usually this quiet at this time in the morning?
Receptionist   It's as busy as can be expected, thank you.
Corin   Did you have a busy night?
Receptionist   We had a comfortable night and we're now resting.
Corin   Have you been put under a lot of pressure by the cuts in the National Health Serivce?

Receptionist	You'll have to talk to the doctor about that, but I'm sure there's nothing to worry about.
Corin	Thank you.

He goes over to Elaine and Conrad.

	May I ask what you're doing here?
Elaine	We've come about the test-tube babies and that.
Conrad	We want a test-tube baby.
Corin	Why, are there problems . . . ?
Elaine	Yes, we've only got a maisonette, so a little tiny test-tube one would be . . .
Corin	No, they grow to a normal size – they're conceived in the test-tube.
Elaine	Well, we'll never both fit in.

Small ward. Consultant sweeps up to woman's bed with group of students.

Corin	*(Voice Over)* It's ten-thirty and time for the consultant's ward round.
Doctor	Good morning, Mrs Jones.
Mrs Jones	Good morning, Doctor.
Doctor	How are we feeling?
Mrs Jones	Not too bad, apart from the agonizing pain.
Doctor	Good, good. You – let's see how much you've picked up. What can you tell me about Mrs Jones?
First student	She's wearing a nightie, Sir.
Doctor	And?
First student	And a bedjacket.
Doctor	You?
Second student	I rather think it's a cardigan.
Doctor	And how would you propose to find out?
Second student	I'd have it X-rayed, Sir.
Doctor	Allinson?
Third student	In view of the danger inherent in repeated X-rays, Sir, I'd prefer to have a period of observation.
Doctor	X-rays, observation – there's a very simple solution to all this. Winstanley?

Fourth student	Ask the patient.
Doctor	Ask the patient! If you want to know something about the patient, ask the patient! Mrs Jones – is that a bedjacket or is it a cardigan?
Mrs Jones	It's a bedjacket, doctor.
Doctor	Gentlemen – it is a bedjacket. Thank you Mrs Jones, and a very good morning to you.

Another ward. Two nurses, Della and Noreen, making a bed.

Corin	What made you want to be a nurse, Della?
Della	It was that telly programme, 'Angels'. Seemed a nice job.
Corin	What particularly attracted you?
Della	The short hours.
Corin	Sorry?
Della	Half an hour, twice a week, seemed too good to be true. Which it was.
Corin	Noreen – what do you like about nursing?
Noreen	The challenge, the teamwork, the sense of responsibility, erm, the feeling that you're helping people, the satisfaction, the nurse–patient relationship and the drugs. Oh – and I quite like the apron.

They smooth the sheets, pleased with the job. An old man's voice comes from under the bed.

Old man	Can I get back in now?
Della	*(shouting down)* No, you stay there Mr Dixon – then the bed stays nice and tidy, all right?
Old man	All right, nurse.

Office of Whizz Kid administrator, very high-tech. He is talking on the phone and checking details on a VDU.

Corin	*(Voice Over)* It's lunchtime, but hospital administrator Kevin Foley wouldn't dream of stopping to eat when there's deals to be done.

Kevin	Mrs Smith? Yes, I'm looking at the figures now – the waiting-list situation – fifteen months for a tonsillectomy, three years for a hip replacement, and five years for two seats in the Upper Circle for 'Cats'. Hip replacement – private? No problem – straight away. In fact there's a special offer this month – buy two hips, get one free. Yes, you can bring your own anaesthetic, though we have to charge corkage. Not at all, nice to do business with you Mrs Smith, *ciaou*.

Puts phone down.

Corin	I hear you've introduced some revolutionary schemes to help the hospital pay for itself?
Kevin	Oh, you heard about that? Yes, I'm glad to say, half of our morgue is now an extremely successful freezer centre.
Corin	Really.
Kevin	Tremendous. You can pop down there, pay your last respects and pick up a very competitive shoulder of lamb at the same time.

Phone rings.

Excuse me.

Recovery room. Noreen shouting at an unconscious man on a trolley.

Corin	*(Voice Over)* It's five-thirty, and here is one of those private patients Kevin Foley is so keen to attract to the hospital. Adam McCalpine is just coming round from the anaesthetic after his operation.
Noreen	Mr McCalpine! Wake up, Mr McCalpine! The operation's over, it's all over, we're taking you back to the ward. Can you hear me?
Man	Mmmm . . .
Noreen	Can you open your eyes for me?
Man	Mmmm . . .
Noreen	And can you give me the number of your Access card?

A corridor. Elaine and Conrad sit outside a door.

Corin	How are you getting on?
Elaine	We've been having tests.
Corin	Fertility?
Elaine	For something, I don't know if it was tility.
Conrad	I had to go in a bathroom with a sexy sort of magazine.
Corin	And how did you get on?
Conrad	I could read most of it.

Hospital entrance. Sirens wailing. Corin stands lit by the blue light of an ambulance. Ambulancemen/women rush by him with a stretcher.

Corin	Eleven-thirty, the pubs are shut, in casualty things are hotting up.

Casualty. Corin goes into a curtained-off cubicle where a drunken man is sprawled on the bed.

Corin	Good evening.
Drunken man	That's very nice, very nice, I say good evening, you say good evening, that's all very nice.
Corin	What's wrong with you exactly?
Drunken man	God knows.
Corin	Are you ill?
Drunken man	I'm as fit as a pig – sorry, talking rubbish . . .
Corin	Why have you come to the hospital?
Drunken man	It's a nice little hospital, isn't it? Don't you agree? I think so, nice little marvellous little . . . nurse!

Nurse enters in a rush with a white coat, which she hands to the drunken man who gets off the bed and puts it on.

Nurse	Sorry – took me ages to find it.

He follows her out.

Now, suspected fractured skull, cubicle nine . . .

Outside the Hospital. Dawn. Same man mopping steps as before.

Corin   *(Voice Over)* Another night is over, and so a new day begins for Kevin and Della and Mrs Jones and Mr McCalpine . . .

Elaine and Conrad come down the steps.

Corin   So what happened, in the end?
Elaine   We didn't get one.
Corin   Didn't get what?
Elaine   A baby! They said you've to wait nine months or something – and the things they wanted us to do!
Conrad   Sections of intercost, or something.
Elaine   It was horrible.
Corin   Well, everybody does it, you know.
Elaine   They don't! Come on, Conrad.

They walk away. Corin stands looking at the hospital. Man waves his mop.

Man   Go on, get out of it! You woolly article!

Kitty: One

Kitty   This wasn't my idea. *(Looks at watch.)* In fact, had it been up to me, I'd have been on my second cream sherry in Kidderminster by now. This lot *(gesturing vaguely and disdainfully around)* – they phoned me up last Thursday. I'd just settled down with a Claire Rayner and a quarter of radishes, so I wasn't best pleased. I said, 'Who is it and keep it brief, because I've a howling draught through my architrave'; and if I'd wanted to freeze to death I'd have gone with Scott to the Antarctic and made a day of it. She said, 'Its Morag from the television programme, do you remember me?' I said, 'Yes, I do; I lent you two cotton buds which I never saw back.' She said, 'I've got the producer for you', so I said, 'I hope you've sealed the envelope properly', which is an old golfing retort of mine. On she comes – the producer – I could hear her boiler-suit creaking even long-distance – 'Is that Kitty?' I said, 'If it's not, this cardigan's a remarkably good fit.' She said, 'Kitty – do you like fun?' I said, 'No, I don't. I had enough of that in 1958 when I got trapped in a lift with a hula-hoop salesman.' She said, 'Would you like to come on our new programme? One of our regulars has a skin complaint and has to spend three months eating peanuts with the light off.'

I said, 'Well, I'm quite pushed busy-wise – I'm doing the costumes for the Rummy Club production of "The Sound of Music", and Helen Murchison's Second Act dirndl is a week's work in itself.' (She claims to be dieting but every time we have 'Doh a Deer a Female Deer' there's a terrible whiff of pear-drops.) But that's by the by-pass.

She said, 'Come to the studios, and we'll thrash it out woman to woman.' Well, she's as much like a woman as Charlie Cairoli, but I just said 'Suit yourself' and rang off.

So I fixed up a lift with Mr Culverhouse in flat nine. Well, he owed me a favour and he has got a very roomy Vauxhall. It was no bother to drop me off because he has an artificial arm from the Western Desert and he was coming through to Roehampton anyway to have his webbing adjusted.

So I turn up – I popped into Marks on my way to return a – well, let's call it an item. I'm ushered into the producer – she hadn't changed – new haircut – if it hadn't been bright blue she'd have been a dead ringer for Stanley Matthews. And she won't wear anything approaching a brassiere – when she plays ping-pong it puts you in mind of something thought up by Barnes Wallis.

Well – she stubs out her Senior Service and she says, 'Kitty, how can we tempt you?' and starts boasting about her big budget. I thought if it's that big, why don't you splash out on some foundation garments but I kept well buttoned. So I stated my terms. One – proper remuneration – I'd seen in the papers about Terry so-called Wogan and his astronomical figure – it wasn't my paper – it was wrapped round a small Savoy at my neighbour's. Two – I want to be chauffeur-driven each way; British Rail having gone completely mad in my opinion, all vertical blinds and chilli con carne – and the driver must be blemish-free – because I'm not coming all the way from Cheadle glued to somebody's carbuncles. Three – I must have a decent dressing-room, and not that cubby-hole next to the chocolate machine. How you're expected to gather your thoughts up to the thud of a falling Bounty I do not know. There's a bit of a dubious silence, and the producer says she'll have to ask upstairs – I thought that's leadership for you – where were you when they bombed Plymouth?

Anyway – we reached a compromise – I got what I wanted and they didn't. I've quite a nice dressing room, I have it Box and Cox with the late-night Vicar. And the chauffeur's called Kent. Kent! I said to him, 'That's not a name, it's a cricket team.'

Anyway – I must go. If we beat the traffic, Mr Culverhouse is taking me for a prawn salad at The Happy Rickshaw. Chinese, but we ask for the other menu. *(Getting up)* Morag! Tuh, there's no laying hands on her now she's engaged . . .

Margery and Joan: Two

Joan   Fascinating as ever, Philippa, and I for one had never really realized how enjoyable and, I may say, hilarious welding could be. Now it's over to Margery for this week's topic of national importance.

Strolls over.

Hello, Margery, what's this week's topic of national importance?

Margery   Hello, Joan. Well, we like to pride ourselves on this programme that we cover areas of concern ignored or even overlooked by the media.

Joan   So what scandal or hitherto unrecognized social problem are we tackling today, Margery?

Margery   Unemployment, Joan.

Joan   Go on Margery, this is fascinating.

Margery   Now I'm not a statistician, Joan.

Joan   And you don't look like one, Margery, quite a bonus.

Margery   But I researched into this pretty thoroughly on my way to the studios this morning, in the mini-cab.

Joan   Because you don't drive, do you Margery?

Margery   No, and so I'm very interested in something we'll be looking at later, which is a specially adapted diesel-powered waterproof armchair.

Joan   But back to the dreary side of life for a moment, Margery. Unemployment – I've never heard of it. What is it?

Margery   I'll deal with that in a moment Joan, but let me tell you this – it affects an awful lot of people.

Joan   How many people, Margery?

Margery   Quite a few, Joan.

Joan   Are we talking about fifty-five-year-old-men in flat caps and bicycle clips, Margery?

Margery   No, we're talking about unemployment. *(Looking round)* Has something been changed? Marion?

Joan So if people are unemployed, and basically that means – what?

Margery It means they haven't got a job – Joan.

Joan Really? As bad as that? Phew. So – I'm unemployed, I haven't got a job, what can I do?

Margery Well of course, there are always lots of jobs advertised in your local paper, and on display at the Job Centre, that's the nice place in the High Street with the orange paint, or if you prefer to work from home – perhaps you have a valuable Afghan hound who can't be left, or cleaning staff you don't trust, then it's worth considering setting yourself up as an investment broker, or writing a best-selling novel.

Joan So basically there's plenty of work about if we're prepared to scout around for it?

Margery Absolutely, Joan.

They stroll over to another part of the set.

Joan And what will you be looking at next week, Margery?

Margery Well, you won't be seeing me next week, because I'll be covered in an operating gown – but you will be seeing my gall bladder which Joan will be removing live in the studio by means of a revolutionary new process so simple it can be performed by a nursing sister, or in an emergency, a qualified librarian.

Joan And I'm particularly looking forward to that, because not only have I never seen a gall bladder, I'm absolutely clueless as to its whereabouts, so I could be getting in quite a pickle.

Lights dim, music in. Joan sits in the armchair and whizzes about. Margery walks off the set.

Margery I'm sorry, I'm going to talk to Marion about this, I'm not happy . . .

Salesman

Living room. Salesman with large samples case, a few
encyclopaedias scattered about, a reluctant woman leafing through
one.

Man   So all in all, these encyclopaedias are a marvellous
investment.

Woman   But I don't think we'd ever –

Man   I'm not saying you're going to read them every day of the
week – but whenever you wanted to refer to them – they'd be
there.

Woman   That's what bothers me – it's that basically they'd be lying
about gathering dust – it's hard enough to keep the house
clean as it is.

Man   *(whipping out 'Dustbuster'-type thing from the case)* In that case,
may I show you this marvellous little gadget? Runs on
re-chargeable batteries, you can do stairs, corners, soft
furnishings, cleavages ha ha *(lunges at her – she fends him off)*.

Woman   No, I'm very happy with my own vacuum cleaner, thank you.

Man   *(whizzing it about)* Dog hairs, nails, it's a remarkable little
machine, it really is.

Woman   No, stop please. No, the house is only difficult to clean
because we're so near the main road, and we get a lot of dust
in through the windows.

Man   *(putting away 'Dustbuster' and getting out double-glazing samples)*
So you're not double-glazed? It's a marvellous investment,
I'm not saying it's cheap, but with what you save in fuel bills,
you'll have made it back in eighty or ninety years, no danger.

Woman   Yes, but how much money are we –

Man   What are you – four bed two recep? At a rough guess and
using our own trained installation engineers, five thousand
eight hundred and seventy-two pounds fifty pence, give or
take.

Woman   That's awfully expensive.

Man	They bring their own tea-bags.
Woman	We can't really –
Man	Or you could install it yourself – I say 'you' – obviously one wouldn't envisage a woman hopping around on scaffolding – don't want someone looking up and catching sight of your panty-bits. But your husband could do it –
Woman	He couldn't really, he has a heart condition.
Man	Has he? That must be a worry to you.
Woman	Well, yes.
Man	*(putting away double-glazing and bringing out insurance leaflets and tables of figures)* Is he insured? If he's, what, forty-five, let's see, if he pays seven, ten, say twelve-pound premium, that's not a lot if you consider the price of fags, if he staggers on till two thousand and thirty-eight, make him ninety-seven-ish, he could pick up somewhere in the region of fifty-eight thousand pounds. And if he kicks the bucket prior to that you get the mortgage paid off, a nice lump sum, a mock crocodile handbag and a slo-cooker.
Woman	He is fully insured, thank you.
Man	Well, how about yourself, women's lib and all that?
Woman	No, I haven't got any –
Man	We've a nice ladies' package going, if you don't smoke and come within the recommended doctor's whatsits. Height?
Woman	Five foot four.
Man	Weight?
Woman	Well, I don't really see that – er –
Man	You ladies! Tut tut tut. A bid of a sweetie gobbler, say no more. It is very easy to let those pounds pile on.
Woman	It certainly is.
Man	But getting them off? Another story. *(He whips out can of diet formula from case.)* You would not believe the fabulous success we're having with this unique liquid diet. You can't get it in the shops – 300 calories a day, all the essential vitamins and minerals you need, plus natural vegetable fibre so no lavatory hang-ups. And you never get bored because it's in a flavour *(He shows her the can)* See? Flavour.
Woman	Well, to be honest – I find this modern-day emphasis on physical appearance rather trivial and pointless – I feel there must be more to life than the everyday here and now . . .
Man	I agree *(putting diet away, bringing out illuminated model of*

	temple and prayer book). That's why I'm so thrilled to be associated with the Holy Temple of the Inner Light plc.
Woman	What is it?
Man	You've heard of the Mormons.
Woman	Oh, yes.
Man	It's a little bit like that, not so many wives, not so many Osmonds.
Woman	It's a religion?
Man	It's whatever it means to you, Mrs King. It's a faith, it's a discipline, it's a way of being. It brings together elements from all the great religions of the world, Buddhism, Judaism, Hindu, the teachings of the Dalai Lama, Mohammed, transubstantiation, reincarnation, druids, naiads, lay-lines – we fuse all these strands into a kind of global mysticism – do you follow me?
Woman	I'm not very well up on comparative religion, I'm appallingly ignorant generally, I just don't know what you're talking about.
Man	In that case, why don't you buy the bloody encyclopaedias!

Reports Local

Serious man at news desk.

Man   And here in our area rioting and unrest continues in the town centre. Earlier today we had reports of windows being smashed and cars overturned. Our report Sally Hardcastle is down there now with a film crew to bring us this report.

Pause – He listens to his earpiece.

I'm sorry – the film crew are still having their lunch – there's been some delay with the moussaka at The Grill and Griddle. Sally Hardcastle is phoning in this report from the scene of the troubles.

Flash up old school photo with Sally's face circled. He picks up his phone.

What's the situation now, Sally?

Sound of pips.

Hello? What's the situation now?

Sally   *(Voice Over)* Hello? Is that the television studios?

Man   Yes, go ahead, Sally.

Sally   Could you put me through to Studio Three, please, I've got a report for Desmond Hambley.

Man   This is Desmond, you're on the air – go ahead.

Sally   Oh hello, Desmond, I didn't recognize your voice – I didn't think we've spoken on the phone before.

Man   What's the news on the riot, Sally?

Sally   I've spoken to your wife, haven't I, about that buggy? *(Pips)* Hang on.

Man   Are you in the middle of the danger area? It sounds pretty noisy.

Sally	No, I'm in Lewis's. I'm in a booth on the second floor, near the Travel Agents'. The noise you can hear is coming from the cafeteria.

A picture comes up of Sally on the phone, a couple of people waiting behind her.

Man	Ah, we have your picture now.
Sally	Yes, John's turned up, but Dennis is still waiting for his pudding. No, we came away from the rioting because it was so noisy.
Man	Is the situation deteriorating?
Sally	Well, as I said, we came away because it was looking a bit nasty. I was worried about my Renault . . .
Man	Are the police planning to move in?
Sally	Well, I haven't really seen any police – lunch took ages, I had to send my chicken back, it was practically pink, then I looked round the sales, so . . .
Man	Have there been any casualties?
Sally	Look, I don't know, I can't really talk now – there's a lady been waiting for ages, and I haven't got any more change – look, I'll pop back to the studios later, shall I? We'll probably have to make a detour because of this awful riot, have you heard about it? Anyway, look, Sally Hardcastle, for Local News, Lewis's, second floor, near the Travel Agents'. Bye!

End on Man's face.

Dr Who

A typical episode; in colour but from no particular period. The doctor and his leggy blonde assistant Fiona (who is wearing a kilt) are running down the usual baco-foil tunnel. Music.

Doctor Hurry, Fiona!
Fiona I can't, Doctor, my stockings are rubbing together.
Doctor In here!

He presses a button on his lapel, which activates the silver-painted up-and-under garage door. They go through the door and stop as they come face-to-face with Crayola at his nerve centre.

Crayola Well, well!
Fiona Who is it, Doctor? I'm not very bright and I haven't got my glasses on.
Doctor It is my old enemy Crayola. Hulloa, Crayola.

Crayola, who has had his back turned to them facing his lousy control panel of blinking lights, turns round. He is the wrinkly sort with the crinkly voice, lots of wires attached everywhere. Hands coming out of some ridiculous part of his body, which is on a caterpillar wheeled trolley. Ears on his chest, mouth on his knee etc.

Crayola Doctor. It's been a long time.
Doctor Aeons.
Crayola As long as that? You don't look a day over five million; how do you do it?
Doctor Table tennis. *(Crayola laughs.)* We don't have much time. I'll keep him talking, you creep round behind him – disconnect his bladdermite tubing and neutralize his thermalobes.
Fiona But Doctor, we haven't got the ming-mongs!
Doctor In that case, I'll creep round behind him and you show him your operation scar.
Crayola *(suddenly ceasing to laugh)* I think not, Doctor.

Fiona Doctor, look out!

Through the up-and-under door come the regulation three guards, two men (one black) and one woman – clingfilm wrapped round their heads, huge ears, bin-liner boiler suits, pointing hairdryers at the doctor.

Crayola Game, set and match I think, Doctor.
Doctor Run for it, Fiona!

They do so; the guards point their hairdryers at him, he freezes and goes negative.

Fiona You've killed him!
Crayola Not at all, my dear. We've merely converted his megaplumfinity into negative kreetathones.
Fiona But what does that mean?

The guards look at each other and shrug.

Guard Search me, dear.

Margery and Joan: Three

Joan And we'll be having more childcare hints from Philippa next week, when she'll be telling us why raw steak and angostura bitters don't make a good meal for your new-born baby. Now it's over to Margery, who's been looking into the ancient and fascinating Japanese art of Bonsai. Hello Margery, you've been looking into the ancient and fascinating Japanese art of Bonsai, haven't you?

Margery Hello, Joan. That's right. With summer fast approaching, we all need to know how to tan our bodies quickly, and more importantly, safely.

Joan is stunned. Silence.

Well, I'm glad you asked me that, Joan – because as you can see, there is a bewildering array of tanning products on the market. I'll just show a few . . .

She holds up products to the wrong camera, so we see them sideways on in long shot. By the time the cameras cut she is holding them out to a different camera so we get a close-up of her sleeves.

Joan *(blankly)* What happened to Bonsai?

Margery Scrapped.

Joan Oh. *(Recovering)* So if I want to get a nice brown tan without burning, how do I go about it, Margery?

Margery The golden rule, Joan – is – build up gradually. The first two weeks of your holiday, stay in your room with a hat and a pullover. And if you've got an old maxi-coat left over from the early seventies – wear that too.

Joan And if I'm sixteen or seventeen, and have never seen a maxi-coat?

Margery If you're sixteen or seventeen, my advice is stay at home and get those qualifications. So to sum up – first two weeks in your room, followed by three or four weeks in a full-length dressing-gown – opening the lapels for a minute or two every other day. Never forget, you can still get a nasty sunburn even at night.

Joan And what about diarrhoea, Margery?

Margery I'm still having it every twenty minutes, Joan.

Joan But you've also been looking at the very latest in household gadgets, haven't you Margery?

Suntan table replaced by another with gadgets on.

Or perhaps you haven't, what do I know.

Margery Yes I have Joan, and a jolly interesting crop they are too. Now I don't use public transport myself, Joan, but a survey out this month shows that a surprisingly awful lot of people do.

Joan And that can lead to problems, can't it, Margery?

Margery That's right, Joan. And one of the worst problems is that at peak periods it's not always possible for a husband and wife to sit together.

Joan So if hubby's down at one end of the bus, with a hair or fluff on the back of his jacket, wifey can't always get near enough to do anything about it.

Margery Or she couldn't. Until this little gizmo came out. (*Picks up telescopic pincer thing:*) She can quietly get this out of her tote-bag, disengage the safety popper, and hey bingo, that offending hair is safely in the ashtray.

Joan Of course one thing about being in a crowd of people is that we can't always be sure of personal daintiness.

Margery That's right, Joan. Now I don't mind jamming a hand into my armpit and sniffing it in public, but some people do; and for them, these musical dress-shields are going to be a real boon. (*Produces ordinary dress-shield with tiny battery and wiring.*)

Joan How do they work, Margery?

Margery Well, I'm pretty whiffy today, so this should show you. Just pop it under my arm here, wait a moment – and if there's any pong at all, this happens. (*It plays a computerized version of 'Eidelweiss'.*) And a lovely melody to boot.

Joan And finally and very quickly, Margery?

Margery Finally and very quickly, Joan – redundancy.

Joan What about it, Margery?

Margery It's upsetting, it's traumatic, but above all, its embarrassing.

Joan So how do we keep it a secret, and stop people recognizing us in the queue at the social security?

Margery Not easy Joan – at least it wasn't – until this little hoo-hah popped up on general release.

She stands up and picks up a kind of shortened Punch and Judy booth.

Light, portable, you can wear this in the dole queue and friends and neighbours will pass you by, none the wiser.

She puts it on over her head, it comes down to waist level.

And when your number's called and you reach the window – *(rolls up a little blind in front of her face)* hey poncho – you can be seen and heard in perfect privacy.

Lights and music.

You'd probably need a bigger size, Joan.

Joan Thanks a buffalo. At least I'm not sniffing my fingers all the day long.

Craft Shop

Arty, hand-woven global village-type gift shop. Arty, hand-woven lady owner watches browsing girl.

Owner   Can I help, or are you just browsing?

Girl   I'm just looking for a present for somebody.

Owner   I see you're looking at the jerseys – they're hand-knitted from the unravelled climbing socks of Lakeland fell walkers.

Girl   Really.

Owner   Yes, if you look closely at the yarn you'll spot the occasional toenail or blister.

Girl   What are these?

Owner   Ukrainian prayer shawls, woven by the mothers of Russian dissidents while in a state of euphoria, which doesn't happen very often, which is why we've only got three.

Girl   How much is the chess set?

Owner   Well, I'm afraid its nine hundred and fifty pounds, but you see it is intricately carved from Lancashire cotton bobbins by disadvantaged Aborigines so –

Girl   Bit expensive.

Owner   We have lots of cheap items – our silk scarves there, two pounds each, all individually dyed using a mixture of beetroot juice, wild grasses and native saliva.

Girl   I can pay a bit more than that . . .

Owner   Perfume? *(Girl takes a whiff of a tester and backs off, blinking.)* That's an aphrodisiac scent, containing rare herbal essences and secretions from the sex glands of the Tibetan mountain rabbit – and we also do that in a drawer-liner.

Girl   It's a house-warming present.

Owner   Oh – how about these Bangladeshi washing stones – I believe you spread the clothes on one, and bang them with the other. I understand it gets them marvellously clean, though it's probably not tremendously good for the buttons.

Girl   Mmmm.

Owner   Stationery? Cards, paper, envelopes – all hand-printed by goats.

Girl   These are nice – what are they?

Owner   Ah – now they're a set of primitive patterning cogs – they're actually for decorating the breasts of Malaysian sacrificial virgins, but I've found them very handy for pastry.

Girl   No, it's all right, thanks – I'll leave it. I really wanted something a bit out of the ordinary.

Kitty: Two

She rushes on with bags and parcels, with her coat on.

Kitty   Now I'm keeping this on because I've got a mad dash to get back to Cheadle. The Rummy Club Sound of Music opens tonight. I'm prompter – and our Mother Superior's on tablets so every other rehearsal it's been 'Climb Every What is it?'

Anyway – reincarnation! The producer set me off on it. She had one of those sessions where you lie back and turn into Florence Nightingale. She reckons she's had three previous incarnations: I think one was a Roman soldier, I forget the other two. Looking at her now, I'd plump for a Sumo wrestler and a bull mastiff. But I'm quite interested in the supernatural. My mother and I once paid out for a seance in Widnes. We wanted to contact my father because we were going camping and we couldn't lay hands on the mallet. This medium – she couldn't have made contact with the other side of a bedside table. She just kept saying she could tell we'd suffered a grievous loss. I said, 'Yes, two pounds each to come in, and our bus fares to Widnes.' But I quite fancied regressing to my earlier lives, so I got Mr Culverhouse to hypnotize me. So I'm lying down – he hasn't got the right sort of watch so he's dangling a rubberized plug – and he counts me back to 1901. 'Who are you', he says. Well everything's dark, but I sense I'm wearing a corset, so that rules out Edward the Seventh. Then suddenly, bang, bang, bang, there's Helen Murchison at the front door assaulting my knocker as per; so it's away with the hypnosis and out with the mixed biscuits.

She'd come round on her way back from giving blood, and why they want it beats me, because the way she eats, it must be 'A' rhesus nougat. She'd come to tell me her daughter was

finally getting married after four years of living in sin just
outside Nantwich. I said 'What's his name?' She said, 'He's
called Nick, and he's very high up in sewage.' I thought, that's
lucky. She said, 'It is a church wedding, but under the
circumstances the bride's opted for knee-length shrimp.' She
tried to impress Mr Culverhouse with her elaborate finger
buffet, but he sees the world for what it is after fifty years in
cocoa. She said if I wanted to give a present, they'd made out
a little list. Little! It made the Domesday Book look like a
raffle ticket. Videos, washing machines – the only thing under
a fiver was a wall-mounted Brillo grip. So they're getting this.
(*She produces an* awful *catering-size coffee tin covered in wallpaper
and ric-rac braid to make a bin.*) I made it! You can't get them
in the shops. I think what makes it is the ric-rac braiding. I
was going to patent it, but I believe there's a lot of hanging
around. Oh, and then she drops another bombshell. She
chomps down the last of the Bourbons and says, 'Kitty – I'm
leaving Bill – we're not compatible.' They never were – he
loves opera, and she can't follow the plot of the Teddy Bears'
Picnic. She only married him because he was pally with a man
who made chocolate misshapes.

Now I must dash – it's curtain-up at seven and these
motorways – they're forever coning you off – I blame the
engineers. You can see them on the hard shoulder, larking
about with their theodolites. (*Gathers her bits together.*) If
anybody's been sitting on my wimples I'll play merry
Hamlet . . .

Wine Bar

Very 'feminine' and 'nice' girl and slightly older man drinking after work in a wine bar.

Man   Cheers.
Girl   Cheers *(drinks)*. Mmm, quite nice and fruity.
Man   They know me here.
Girl   Really? Because some white wines – they can sort of make you scrunch your bottom up, can't they? But this is quite cordial, isn't it?
Man   Do you think you're going to enjoy working for the company?
Girl   Oh, yes. It's a very choice powder-room, ever such unusual washbasins, quite opaque.
Man   That's a very attractive dress, if I may say so.
Girl   Oh, do you like it? I think it makes me look a bit extinct, do you know what I mean? I like the fabric, though, it's quite commercialized.
Man   Do you have a boyfriend, or . . . ?
Girl   No, I don't really like steady relationships – they make me feel a bit Rice Krispie-ish, do you know what I mean?
Man   Because I'd very much like to take you out one evening, if I may.
Girl   I don't think so.
Man   Because I'm married?
Girl   I don't really like going out with people from work – it all gets sort of conjugated.
Man   Nobody has to know.
Girl   It always does get out, though. Offices are really ostentatious for gossip, aren't they?
Man   Well, it wouldn't matter, would it?
Girl   Well, it's against company policy, isn't it? People going out with their secretaries. There might be a big sort of moussaka about it.
Man   Yes, but what would be the worst that could happen?
Girl   Well, the worst that could happen would be that Head Office found out and I had to fire you, Colin. Cheers.

Margery and Joan: Four

Joan *(in neck brace and knee-length plaster)* And as Philippa climbs out of that piranha tank, I'm sure she won't mind if I let you into a little secret – she's actually into the fourth week of a very serious nervous breakdown! Now it's over to Margery, who's been finding out what's available holiday-wise for those of us who aren't going abroad this summer. Hello Margery, what's available holiday-wise for those of us who aren't going abroad this summer?

Margery Hello, Joan. Well believe it or not, but not every holiday-maker will be flying to Marbella or Alicante with a suitcase full of velour leisure shorts singing 'Y Viva España'.

Joan And why is that, Margery?

Margery Possibly because they don't know the words to the second verse, Joan.

Joan So a lot of people will be looking for a reasonably priced package in this country?

Margery That's right, Joan.

Joan OK – so I'm single, I don't have very much money, I can't afford to go abroad, I don't make friends easily, what can I do?

Margery Look, we had all this out in the wine bar . . . *(Realises her mistake.)* Well, there's lots of alternatives available, Joan, the cheapest being a two-week conservation holiday in the West Midlands dragging old bedsteads out of the Grand Union Canal and living on pulses.

Joan And what will I need to take with me?

Margery Well, if they haven't been soaked – a can of air-freshener.

Joan And if I'm a book-lover and would like nothing better than to meet my favourite authors?

Margery Then hie yourself along to the Swan Hotel, Warwick, where you can mingle with popular novelists and have the chance to examine such literary treasures as the original manuscript of *Wuthering Heights*, James Herriot's collection of rubber gloves, and most exciting of all – Jeffrey Archer's very first bank statement.

Joan   But you've also been looking at Singles Holidays, haven't you, Margery?

Margery   That's right, Joan. Because for every outgoing popular physically attractive swinger like me, there's an emotionally repressed lumpy old pongo like Joan. See how we got on.

Cut to film

A coach bowling along a cliff road.

Joan   *(Voice Over)* Margery and I are heading for the three-star Cliff Top Hotel – where single people of all sexes are hoping for sun, fun and a little bit of mountaineering.

Front of Hotel. Coach. Joan on the steps of the coach. Extras collecting luggage at back. Margery seen through the coach window heaving into a sick bag.

Joan   *(to camera)* Well, a bumpy five-hour drive on badly tarmacked B roads wouldn't suit everybody. *(Margery appears behind Joan, wiping her mouth.)* But we're both raring to pick up our bags and get going.

Walks to rear of coach. Margery picks up the last case.

   (as rehearsed) The blue samsonite, please.

Driver   *(closing the boot)* Nope, that's the lot – sorry.

Twin-bedded room. Margery holding up racy evening clothes against herself and chucking them on the bed.

Joan   *(on other bed)* Well, I've been told my case will be here in the morning, so till then, Margery and I will be sharing the same toothbrush.

Margery   *(to herself)* That's what you think.

Joan   *(checking timetable)* Well, it's six o'clock, so I'm heading for the TV lounge, for the first event of Singles Week – a Twist 'n'

Jive session with the Pauline Mowbray Skiffle Experience.
Coming, Margery?

Margery No thanks. I'm going to the bar.

Bar. Joan leaning up at the bar. Everyone very jolly. Waiter serves Joan a cocktail and moves out of shot.

Joan Well, after a few of the hotel's speciality cocktails, the ice is well and truly broken. Everyone's having a marvellous time! Over to you, Margery. Cheers!

Another part of the bar. Camera finds Margery performing a drunken dance with a reluctant businessman who's trying to get away.

Margery You don't need to phone your wife! Come on – forty-two and no bra, not bad, eh?

Back to Joan, immersed in her cocktail.

Joan And I might try that later in the week! Now it's off to bed, because believe you me, tomorrow's going to be a very full day!

Poolside. Joan in towelling robe and extremely elaborate swimming cap.

Joan Well, I've been shopping, I've visited the local museum and I'm just recovering from a vigorous session of poolside aerobics, and I imagine that Margery's been pretty busy as well. *(Waves up at a balcony)* Yoo-hoo! Margery!

Margery on a balcony wrapped in a sheet, having been 'at it' all night and just woken up. All messy hair and smudged eye-shadow.

Margery *(can't think or speak)* Hello, Joan. Yes – er – I've been pretty busy. *(Yawns.)* You know . . .

The businessman in towel stomps out on the balcony from the room, grabs a pair of underpants and goes back in, mumbling.

Man　　Can't find your pants.
Margery　What? *(Yawns.)*

Cliff face. Joan is half-way up the cliff dangling on a rope held by Margery, who has reached the top. Both are in full climbing gear. Margery still not with it.

Joan　　Well, this is the highlight of the holiday as far as I'm concerned, a two-day course in simple mountaineering. It's a marvellous way for single people to get to know each other, because in a life-and-death situation like this, you're totally dependent on your climbing partner *(tugs the rope)*. Margery, I'm coming up!
Margery　*(yawning)* OK.
Joan　　*(starting to climb)* If Margery was to let her concentration lapse for just one second, I could literally –

She falls out of shot.

Back to the studio. Joan in neck brace as before.

Margery　Well, that's it – and happy holidays!
Joan　　Bye!

Music. Lights fade.

Margery　When are they taking the pins out?
Joan　　They're not.
Margery　Bad luck.

*Acorn
Antiques*

Episode One

*Scene One. A tiny set, very artificial looking. An antique shop.
Through the back door is a kitchen, with the end of a draining
board and then a gap where the flattage has run out. Outside
the shop window is a crooked photo of a street. All the actors in
this serial are over made-up (women) or speak ironically (men).
Babs is blonde, sitting by a blank wall-plan. She's on the
phone, holding it well away from her face for the camera.
Music.*

Babs   Acorn Antiques, can I help you? No, I'm afraid he's out
buying antiques, who is it calling?

*Mrs Overall, the daily help, comes in with coffee. Babs waves
and smiles, then frowns abruptly.*

Rowena? From Kuwait? Hello? Hello?

She puts the phone down.

Darn. Oh sorry, Mrs Overall.

Mrs Overall Here's your coffee, Miss Babs. Now what's wrong?

Babs   Oh nothing, just rather a mysterious phone call from the
Far East.

Mrs Overall Yes, well, sometimes that's God's way of saying think on
and look sharp.

Babs   You're right. Gosh. I am awful. Here I am blabbing away
about my own troubles and I never asked you about your
husband's car crash.

Mrs Overall Oh he's dead, Miss Babs. In fact I was going to ask you if
I could have a couple of hours off on Thursday for the
funeral.

Babs   Of course. Just pop back at five for the hoovering. What
happened?

Mrs Overall His heart stopped beating.

Babs	Oh, no.
Mrs Overall	Yes, well, sometimes that's God's way of telling you you're dead. Not to worry, Bingo tonight. Mr Kenneth not down yet?
Babs	Er, no.
Mrs Overall	That's not like him, he's not having a nervous breakdown, is he?
Babs	To tell you the truth, Mrs Overall, we had a huge row last night, he put the triplets in the Wolsely and I haven't seen him since.
Mrs Overall	Men! Oh well, better get on and dust a few antiques.

Babs sips coffee and pulls a face.

Babs	Well, they say things go in threes.
Mrs Overall	Why, whatever's happened?
Babs	You forgot my sweeteners. Ho ho ho.
Mrs Overall	Ho ho ho.

They laugh.
Music.

Scene Two. Babs on the phone.

Babs	Yes, just bring your antiques in. Bye.

Enter an enigmatic man (Clifford).

Clifford	Babs?
Babs	Bored with Zurich, or did Zurich get bored with you?
Clifford	You always did ask a good question.
Babs	But did I ever get a good answer?
Clifford	You look well. Answering the phone in a family antiques business seems to suit you.
Babs	Thank you, kind sir.
Clifford	Babs, can't we . . . ?

Babs	We? Who's we, Clifford? There might have been a we before you left me by the handbags in a well-known store . . .

Pause.

Clifford	Don't say any more. I love you, Babs.
Babs	I've changed, Clifford. I have triplets now.

He lunges at her over the desk.

Clifford	Darn your triplets!

He kisses her, the desk cracks ominously. They corpse silently while kissing.
Music.
Credits.
We cut back to close-up of Clifford.

There's something I haven't told you. I go bell-ringing on Wednesday nights.

Episode Two

Scene One. Babs as before on the telephone.

Babs	As I say, it certainly sounds like a genuine Picasso, Martin, but I would have to see it to be sure. Bye.

She looks at the phone and puts it down, smiling. Enter Berta, a Babs look-alike, but brunette where Babs is blonde.

Berta! You look marvellous! So you're out of intensive care!

Berta	I told Doctor Spencer I had to get back and help you out in the shop, so he cured me. So here I am. Ha Ha Ha.

They laugh.

Babs	Coffee, or are you still on your diet?
Berta	Oh, diet be blowed! Ha ha.
Babs	Mrs Overall!

She enters immediately.

Mrs Overall	Well, if it isn't Miss Berta!
Berta	Hello, Mrs O. How's widowhood treating you?
Mrs Overall	Mustn't grumble. I sometimes think being widowed is God's way of telling you to come off the pill.
Berta	Still the same Mrs O!
Mrs Overall	Well, this coffee won't get made on its own.

They all pause, realising a line has been missed.

Babs	Oh yes, two coffees, thank you.
Berta	No milk for me.
Mrs Overall	Well, this coffee won't get made on its own.

Exit Mrs Overall.

Babs	And a plate of your delicious home-made gingerbread, please. Bet you didn't get that in intensive care.
Berta	Oh, I don't know. Money talks, even in hospital, Babs. And though of course it was a dreadful shame Daddy being shot like that in Dhaka, being a millionairess does have its compensations.

Enter Mrs Overall with a tray full of scummy coffee and biscuits.

Mrs Overall	Here we are. It's awfully quiet in here. Anybody would

	think you were talking about million-pound legacies or something.
Babs	Good heavens, no.
Berta	Oh, come on, Babs. Mrs O's practically one of the family. Daddy's gone and got himself shot in Dhaka, Mrs O.
Mrs Overall	Oh, and he'd only just got over that chill on his kidneys. Well, you know what I think?
Berta	What?
Mrs Overall	I think you better have some milk in your coffee after all! Ha ha.
Berta	I think I had! Ha ha.

They laugh.

Scene Two. Babs and Berta poring over blank papers at the desk.

Berta	Yes, that's much better. If we deliver these antiques on Friday morning, we can take delivery of these antiques in the afternoon.

Babs nods, having no dialogue but waiting for someone to enter. Enter Derek, the handyman.

Derek	Excuse me, Miss Babs and Miss Berta, could I have a word?
Babs	Well, if it's to ask me for another job for your untrustworthy cousin Jacob, then the answer's no. His last little escapade cost me thirty-two pounds in French polish. Not to mention apologising to every Asian grocer between here and Manchesterford.
Derek	No, it's not that – it's your father, Miss Berta, he's been seen in the Post Office.
Berta	But my father's dead!

Music.
Credits.
Back to close-up of Derek.

Derek   He was buying a TV licence stamp and a padded envelope.

Episode Three

Scene One. Trixie is on the phone. She is very flighty and tarty.

Trixie   No, I'm sorry, Miss Babs has taken the triplets to see 'Get Carter', they won't be back till this afternoon. No, you won't recognise my voice, this is my first day in the antique shop, I've just been moved up from antique packing. Sorry? Trixie. Trixie Trouble, some people call me. Bye . . .

Mrs Overall enters disapprovingly with a cocktail and some biscuits.

Mrs Overall Here's your cocktail, and don't blame me if you run out of stomach lining.

Trixie   I won't. Anyway, I only have to snap my fingers and somebody I know will come running with a dozen stomach linings.

Mrs Overall I suppose you mean Mr Kenneth?

Trixie   He's already bought me a leotard and a wet-look wig.

Mrs Overall And what did you have to do in return?

Trixie   You'd better ask the receptionist at the Formica Motel.

Mrs Overall Disgusting. And him an ex-Territorial with triplets.

Trixie   That's a matter of conjecture. I found out quite a few things at the Formica Motel; one, that your precious Miss Babs checked in there nine months to the day before the triplets were born.

Mrs Overall Who with?

Enter Derek. Trixie files her nails pointedly.

Derek	It's very quiet in here, I hope you weren't talking about me.

Scene Two. Babs at the desk with Derek.

Babs	Right, so we'll have those antiques packed up immediately and sent down to the station. Plenty of Sellotape, we don't want any more accidents.
Derek	Yes, Miss Babs.
Babs	*(over-casually)* How's your girlfriend these days, Derek? What was her name, Marie-Thérèse Francine Dubois?
Derek	Yes, Miss. She's – back in the convent, Miss.
Babs	Oh, no! After all that trouble you went to, to find her a pleated skirt. Did she leave a note?
Derek	She left a novel, but I don't think it's very commercial.

They speak together.

	Miss Babs!
Babs	Derek!
Derek	I still think about you, Miss Babs. When I'm watching the show-jumping or grilling a tomato.

She puts out a hand and snatches it back as Trixie enters. They all crowd into one shot.

Trixie	Oh, sorry. Hope I'm not interrupting anything.
Babs	Of course not, Trixie. We were just discussing the best way of packing a Spode tea service.
Trixie	Yes, well, we can't afford to have anything broken, can we?
Babs	What do you mean?
Trixie	Like your marriage to Mr Kenneth?

She pulls out some photos from her bag.

Trixie   It's amazing what you can find in a waterproof packet tied to a lavatory ballcock if you look hard enough.

She tosses them down on the table. Reaction.
Music.
Credits.

Seems like I'm not the only one round here with a birthmark shaped like a moped – Mummy . . .

Episode Four

Scene One. Trixie and Mrs Overall at the desk.

Mrs Overall   Well it's a long time since I've seen a diamond engagement ring as expensive as that. Not since Miss Babs got married.

Trixie   Why, this is her ring, Mrs O! Don't forget we just found out Miss Babs is my mother!

Mrs Overall   Why, of course. But doesn't that mean you're engaged to your own brother?

Trixie   Well, yes, but Mummy spoke to the vicar and he's prepared to make an exception.

Mrs Overall   That's a relief. Well, I'd better go and take away Miss Babs's coffee cup. It's a new brand, the last lot tasted a little bit odd apparently.

Enter Babs.

Babs   Hello, Mrs O. I thought I'd bring my own coffee cup down today. You know, it still tastes a little bit odd.

Trixie   What sort of little bit odd?

Babs   Oh, I don't know, almost as if someone was trying to kill me . . .

Trixie	Oh Mum, you are an old silly billy – ho ho.

She stops laughing when she notices Babs and Mrs Overall look serious.

Babs	Well, you see, I am the majority shareholder in Acorn Antiques, since Berta's amnesia. If I were to die that would certainly suit Cousin Jerez very well.
Mrs Overall	But he's a notorious gambler and playboy. And anyway, he's in Marbella.

Enter Cousin Jerez with a peculiar accent.

Jerez	Correction, *was* in Marbella. Planes are very quick nowadays, or perhaps here in your world of antiques you did not know this.
Mrs Overall	I'll make some sherry, Miss Babs. *(Exits.)*

Babs corpses slightly at this mistake.

Jerez	And who is this charming young señorita?
Babs	She's my daughter, and she's engaged.
Jerez	Not too engaged to come out dancing this evening, I hope?
Trixie	I, I . . .
Babs	Aren't you and Bobby going crown green bowling this evening?
Trixie	No, he's ricked his wrist. Yes, I'd love to come out dancing.
Jerez	That's settled, then.
Trixie	Can I borrow your long-line bra, Mummy?
Babs	It's in my sideboard.
Jerez	Do you have any dance dresses that fasten with velcro?
Trixie	Yes, a blue one.
Jerez	Wear it.

Reaction from Babs.

Scene Two. The lounge. A sofa and a standard lamp. Babs and Jerez are having coffee.

Jerez   That was a delicious five-course meal, thank you. I'd forgotten how good you were with quails.

Babs   I may feed you, Cousin Jerez, but I don't like you. Let's cut the pleasantries, shall we? Just why do you want to buy my shares? You don't like antiques and you never have done.

Jerez   True. But I do like motorway service stations.

Babs   What do you mean?

Jerez   Look out of the window.

Babs   There are some council workmen putting a sign up. I can't quite . . . 'New motorway to be built here, starting the 25th'. That's tomorrow! Why haven't I had a letter?

Jerez whistles a few notes.

Why are you whistling like that? I know that tune, it's the one our postman always whistles. Oh I see, it wasn't a postman at all, it was you!

Enter Mrs Overall.

Mrs Overall   Can I clear away now, Miss Babs? The triplets are a bit fractious and I promised I'd pop up and read them a bit of Simone de Beauvoir.

Babs   Yes, do clear away, Mrs O. In fact, you may as well clear away the whole darn shop!

Music.
Credits.

Jerez   Could you fetch my briefcase, Mrs Overall? I'd like to show Miss Babs my theodolite.

Episode Five

Scene One. Derek puffing and panting, having just moved something. Enter Mrs Overall with tea.

Mrs Overall Here's your beef tea, Derek. You've never shifted that 1869 Bechstein all by yourself?

Derek Well, I didn't like to bother Mr Kenneth. He was having his breakfast.

Mrs Overall What was it Muesli? What was it, muesli?

Derek I think so, Mrs O.

Mrs Overall Yes well, I think muesli is God's way of making shredded wheat look exciting.

Derek winces.

It's your heart, isn't it, Derek? You strained it, didn't you, lifting that oil tanker off Miss Berta's handbag?

Derek Well, I knew she was right fond of it. Do you think those revolutionary new tablets will cure her amnesia?

Mrs Overall Well they might, if she could ever remember to take them.

Pause. Enter Trixie in a wedding dress.

Trixie Honestly, I could kill those triplets!

Mrs Overall shakes her head. Trixie realizes it's not her entrance and retreats, bumping into Babs.

Babs Hello Derek, Mrs O. Honestly, I just don't see how we can get this wedding ready in a month. Trixie hasn't even chosen her dress yet.

Derek What's happened about the new motorway, Miss Babs?

Babs Oh, I phoned up the Town Hall and they've agreed to re-route it and knock some poor people's houses down instead.

Mrs Overall Oh, I am pleased. This calls for some tonic wine and a sponge finger.

Babs Yes, Mrs O. I should jolly well think it does.

They all laugh. Derek winces and holds his chest.

I say Derek, your heart's strong enough to put the marquee up all by yourself, isn't it?

Derek If it's for an Acorn Antiques wedding, Miss Babs, I'll put it up even if it kills me.

Mrs Overall and Babs look apprehensive.

Scene Two. The lounge. Berta and Babs on the sofa. Trixie rushes in as before, in a clean wedding dress.

Trixie Honestly, I could kill those triplets!

Babs Calm down, Trixie, whatever's the matter?

Trixie They've put jammy fingerprints all over the front – all over it at the back.

Babs We'll get Mrs O to sponge it off.

Mrs Overall enters as she is being called for.

Mrs O!

Mrs Overall What on earth's wrong with the front of your frock? Looks like jam.

Trixie On the back, yes.

Mrs Overall *(out of character)* What?

Trixie There is jam on the back. The triplets didn't put any on the front.

Mrs Overall freezes, completely lost.

Shall I come along with you and you'll find something to sponge it with?

Mrs Overall Come along with me and I'll find something to sponge it with.

After a short pause, they leave the room.

Babs   Trixie's going to look gorgeous this afternoon, isn't she, Berta?

Berta   I don't know any Trixies.

Laughs slightly at this odd remark.

I don't know anybody. I live in a world of strangers.

Enter Clifford.

Babs   Clifford! What are you doing here? I thought I made my feelings quite clear last November in the British Home Stores.

Clifford   But I'm here to see Berta.

Babs   Berta? But you hardly know her.

Clifford   You may well be right, Babs, but the fact remains, whether she can remember it or not, Berta and I were married by the Bishop of Manchesterford the Tuesday before last.

Music.
Credits.

Babs   So that's why there was confetti on her body-warmer!

Episode Six

Scene One. Clifford, face unmarked, is mopping his nose with a bloodstained hanky. Berta and Babs stand by, faces blank. They receive some cue and begin acting.

Babs   Well, Clifford, you came in at exactly the right moment.

	Trust me to forget Cousin Jerez was an expert knife-thrower.
Clifford	He won't be building any more motorways round here in a hurry.
Babs	What's in your letter, Berta?
Berta	It's from the Bishop of Manchesterford. No, I can't have an annulment, and yes, I did leave my gardening gloves in the vestry.

Short pause. Enter Mrs Overall.

	Hear that, Mrs O?
Berta	Look Mrs O, no amnesia!
Mrs Overall	Oh, I am pleased.
Berta	And do you know what was the first thing I remembered, what it was?
Mrs Overall	No, I don't, Miss Berta.
Berta	I remembered that I'm absolutely mad about your delicious home-made gingerbread!

They all laugh.

Mrs Overall	Coming right up, Miss Berta.
Clifford	Could Berta and Babs fetch it themselves, Mrs O? I'd, er, like a word.
Babs	Why, of course we could. As Mrs O would say, fetching your own gingerbread is God's way of letting you have an extra piece!

Babs and Berta exit laughing. As Clifford speaks Babs knocks into something off the set.

(Babs	What blithering nuisance left that here?)
(Voice	Ssh!)
Clifford	There's been a new development over Berta's father's will. A new one has been found, dated the day he died . . .
Mrs Overall	And who's the sole beneficiary this time?

Clifford	That's the problem. It's a little redhead he met in the blackout in 1943. They had one night of passion and he never saw her again.
Mrs Overall	Or he thought he never saw her again!
Clifford	What do you mean, Mrs O?
Mrs Overall	Oh, I'm grey now, Mr Clifford, fairly grey indeed, but right up to 1947 my hair was red – as red as a London bus!

Music.

Scene Two. The lounge. A celebration. Mrs Overall, Trixie, Derek, Babs, Berta and Clifford, all drinking water out of champagne glasses.

Berta	I can't believe Mrs O is my mother!
Mrs Overall	Well, I am. The doctor said he'd never seen a finer pair of twins.
Berta	Twins? But –
Mrs Overall	A lovely big boy.
Berta	But where is he now?
Mrs Overall	I had to give him away – we hadn't room for the two cots.
Babs	Oh well, he probably would have turned into a hulking great brute anyway.

She stares at Derek thoughtfully.

Trixie	Oh I spoke to our family doctor, Doctor Wimley, today.
Babs	And?
Trixie	Apparently, being spiteful and having lots of extra-marital affairs could bring back my jaundice, so I'm going to be really nice from now on.
Clifford	So we can't call you Trixie Trouble any more.
Trixie	No, in fact its Sister Trixie – I've taken holy orders. Bobby's running me up to the convent in the Wolseley. Bye!

Exit Trixie. The phone rings.

Babs   Hello? I thought you'd committed suicide. OK, see you later. That was my so-called husband, not dead at all. He says put the triplets in their body-warmers – he's taking us all to Manchesterford Zoo, if you please!

Mrs Overall   It was just a cry for help, Miss Babs. Otherwise why try to slash your wrists with an electric razor?

Babs   I'd better go and find that king-size thermos. Looking at animals can be thirsty work.

Berta   Oh, we'll go and look for it, Babs.

Clifford   Yes, Berta and I have lots to talk about.

Mrs Overall   Well, if it's to be another christening, I'll need plenty of notice, or we won't have nearly enough delicious home-made gingerbread.

Berta   We will!

Clifford and Berta leave, laughing.

Babs   She may find my thermos, but will she ever find her twin brother?

Mrs Overall   All I know is, he's called Derek and he's a handyman in an antiques shop.

Babs   Derek? That's your name, isn't it, Derek?

Derek   Well, yes, Miss Babs.

Babs   And this is an antiques shop and you are a handyman!

Derek   I must be Miss Berta's twin brother then, Miss Babs.

Babs   Yes, run along and tell her, Derek!

Exit Derek.

Babs   Phew – it's been an . . . Sorry, Mrs O, both talking at the same time there.

Mrs Overall   I was just saying, someone had better answer that phone.

Phone begins to ring.

Babs   Oh blow, I suppose I'd better answer it.

Mrs Overall You answer it and I'll bring you a nice hot cup of coffee.

Babs   You don't have to.

Phone stops ringing.

After all, you are the sole proprietor of Acorn Antiques now. Hello?

Mrs Overall leaves.

The 'Mona Lisa'? Yes, I certainly have heard of it. Yes do, we're open till five. Bye.

Mrs Overall comes back in with coffee.

Looks like we won't have to go out of business after all. I've just been offered Leonardo da Lisa's 'Mona Vinci' at a very reasonable price.

Mrs Overall And Miss Berta's found your thermos, and apparently it's not a thermos at all, it's a very valuable Georgian silver wine cooler!

Babs   Well, they say things go in threes.

Mrs Overall Why, whatever's the third thing?

Babs   You remembered my sweeteners! Ho ho.

They laugh.
Music.
Credits.

Mrs Overall Oh Miss Babs, I'm awfully sorry, I think I've given you the wrong coffee – that one's full of poison guaranteed to cause agonizing death within minutes!

Reaction from Babs

Episode Seven

---

*Film. Ext. Day. Village High Street. Small van labelled
'Acorn Antiques' pulls up in front of a shop bearing no
resemblance to the one in the studio. The shop has been hastily
and badly re-named 'Acorn Antiques', but the real name of the
shop can be seen underneath. Miss Babs gets out of the van,
holding an antique, goes over on her ankle as she steps down,
and goes into the shop. Small group of interested onlookers
nearby stare at the camera throughout.*

---

*Scene One. Shop as before. Babs selling an antique to our extras
as before. She hands over a large paper bag (printed with 'Acorn
Antiques') and some change.*

Babs   And fifty-three change. Bye!

Extras leave. Phone rings.

Acorn Antiques, can I help you? Gainsborough's Blue
Boy? Yes, I think we have it in mauve, I'll just check.

Flips over blank bits of paper.

Yes, we do; shall I pop it under the counter for you? Not
at all, bye!

Puts phone down. Enter Mrs Overall with tray of coffee.

Mrs Overall   Here's your coffee, Miss Babs.
Babs   Thanks Mrs O, no poison this time I hope.
Mrs Overall   Yes, I'm sorry about that – attempting to murder you was
just a silly way of trying to draw attention to myself. I

shan't need to do it again now you've bought me this
lovely blouse.

*Babs smiles absently and then sighs. Mrs Overall misses the
cue, Babs sighs again, more obviously.*

Mrs Overall	Why, whatever's the matter, Miss Babs? Have you got an incurable disease, or is it just the sterilized milk?
Babs	I wish it were.
Mrs Overall	Then what on earth –
Babs	I won't beat about the bush, Mrs O. Ever since Mr Kenneth left to become a follower of that weird religious sect, Acorn Antiques has been losing money. And this letter you were just asking me about is to Dorcas and Hincaster.
Mrs Overall	The Manchesterford estate agents?
Babs	Yes. Pop it into the pillar box on the corner immediately, Mrs O – Acorn Antiques is going up for sale!

Mrs Overall goes out of the door.

Music.

---

*Cut to film. Ext. Day. Street. Mrs Overall, now miraculously
attired in coat and hat, comes out of the shop, walks to the post
box, takes from the pocket of her coat an entirely
different-looking letter, stares at it meaningfully and puts it
back in her pocket. All this is watched by gawpers in distance.*

---

*Scene Two. Living room. Babs and Clifford. He is snuggling
up to Babs on the settee. She is unresponsive.*

Clifford   What's wrong, Babs? Last night you were so warm and
passionate . . .

Babs	Last night was yesterday, Clifford. I was happy, we had champagne, we danced . . .
Clifford	You danced – magnificently . . .
Babs	Oh, anyone can do the can-can.
Clifford	Not in a snack bar.

As suddenly as he can, Clifford goes down on one knee.

Babs!

A beat late, Mrs Overall enters.

Mrs Overall	There's a visitor, Miss Babs. *(Mumbles absently)* Oh Mrs O.
Babs	Oh, Mrs O, can't you see we're busy?

Cliffords gets up, annoyed.

Mrs Overall	But this is important.
Clifford	*This* is important.
Mrs Overall	*(as herself)* Yes, 'this is important', I said that, didn't I?
Babs	Clifford was about to ask me a very important question, Mrs O.
Mrs Overall	In that case, I'll wait outside.

Mrs Overall goes out.

Clifford	Babs – will you marry me?
Babs	Of course, Clifford, but do you know what you're taking on?
Clifford	A loveable scatterbrain with the nicest lipstick in Manchesterford.
Babs	Lipstick – and debts.
Clifford	Debts?
Babs	Quite frankly, Clifford, I'm flat, flat broke.
Clifford	But you gave me oysters.
Babs	Instant mashed potato and a heck of a lot of nail varnish.

But money doesn't matter, Clifford. *(Turns round and sees he's gone – or nearly gone)* Clifford? Clifford?

Enter Mrs Overall.

Mrs Overall Oh Miss Babs, you've never been jilted again.
Babs I think I jolly well have, Mrs O.
Mrs Overall Men! If they're not doing that they're becoming world heavyweight boxers.
Babs Oh – who was the visitor?
Mrs Overall It was your wicked cousin Jerez, Miss Babs, completely reformed and doing a sandwich course in computer studies at Fuengirola Poly. He dropped in to see if you wanted twenty-five thousand pounds to boost your flagging antiques business.
Babs Twenty-f– I could fill the place with antiques for that, and fit a new cistern in the downstairs cloakroom into the bargain! Well, where is Cousin Jerez, Mrs O – bring him in!

Music.
Credits (list of credits to end with antiques adviser – Rosamund Crull).

Mrs Overall Oh, he couldn't wait, Miss Babs. I told him you were having a proposal done and he caught the next plane back to Marbella!

Episode Eight

Scene One. The shop. Babs, Jerez and Mrs Overall laughing on cue.

Babs But what I can't understand is why Dorcas and Hincaster –

Mrs Overall	The Manchesterford estate agents, yes?
Babs	Why they never put Acorn Antiques on the property market.
Mrs Overall	Because I never posted the letter.
Babs	So they never got the letter at all.
Mrs Overall	No – because I never posted it.
Jerez	Well, that is too complicated for a simple Spaniard like me, but as they say, All's Well *(The other two are supposed to join in with the second half of this, but aren't sure when to come in)* That Ends Well!
Babs	That ends well.
Mrs Overall	All's well that ends well. Well, this calls for a cup of delicious home-made coffee.
Jerez	Home-made coffee? I'm afraid I do not –
Mrs Overall	Well, we have been economizing and this is Acorn Antiques – so what do you think I've been making the coffee out of?
Babs	I give in.
Mrs Overall	Antiques!

Exit Mrs Overall, laughing. Stops laughing abruptly, and clears throat.

Babs	But seriously, Cousin Jerez – it was marvellous of you to lend me the money – are you sure you don't want anything in return?
Jerez	I would like, how do you say in the English – to marry you.
Babs	Well, that's not quite the correct jargon, but I do get your drift. I'm sorry, Jerez, it's not possible.

Jerez whips round and bangs his face on a camera.

Jerez	Ow. What are you sayin' to me?
Babs	When I married Mr Kenneth I gave birth to three children, all born on the same day, all triplets – two of them had dangerously straight hair and had to be rushed immediately to the hairdressers, nurses worked day and

night with curling tongs and heated rollers – and if that's what marriage entails, then quite frankly Cousin Jerez, the answer's no, no –

Mrs Overall opens the door and closes it again.

The answer's no, no, no!

Music.

Cut to film. The shop. Jerez comes out, slams the door, hails a taxi. There is no sound. Clifford collides with him, catapulting from behind the camera.

Scene two. The shop. The door is now open. Enter Mrs Overall with coffee.

Mrs Overall Whatever was that terrible bang?
Babs Cousin Jerez slamming the door. The Spaniards may have enormous onions, but their manners leave a lot to be desired.
Mrs Overall And their football's deteriorated since the World Cup, if you ask me. *(Pause.)* So no fat cheque.
Babs In other words, Mrs O, we're right back to square –

Enter Clifford.

Clifford One?
Babs Clifford! But –
Clifford Our friend Jerez seemed in rather a hurry. *(Takes out a piece of paper labelled 'Jerez – cheque'.)* Certainly he never noticed I'd taken this from his overcoat pocket.

(Jerez wasn't wearing an overcoat, at least not in the film.)

Babs The cheque! Quick, Mrs O, it's three twenty-five, take it

83

	to the local branch of the nearest bank and cash it immediately!
Mrs Overall	I certainly will, Miss Babs. *(Setting off)* And on my way back, I'll buy us some ginger bourbons and a lovely new cistern for the downstairs cloakroom.
Babs	You do that.
Clifford	Hey! Don't forget the cheque *(throws a paper dart)*. Catch!

It goes nowhere near her. We hear an urgent voice off saying 'Leave it, just go.' Exit Mrs Overall.

Thought any more about marrying me?

Music.
Credits.

Babs	I can never marry Clifford – I have a terrible disease. I'm allergic to men's pyjamas. One whiff of a pyjama jacket – even a pocket of a pyjama jacket – and I could literally drop – down – dead!

Episode Nine

Scene One. Shop. Babs on the phone. Extras as usual.

Babs	Hello – Acorn Antiques, can I help you? I'm sorry – you'll have to speak up – we're having extensive alterations and drastic refurbishments.

Sound of half-hearted laughing.

No, we're sticking with mauve. Look – I'll have to go, Mrs Overall's standing over me with a cup of coffee. Bye!

Babs puts phone down. Mrs Overall catapults in with coffee.

Mrs Overall	I've been standing here so long this coffee's practically congealified!
Babs	Oh Mrs O, nobody would think you had a degree in linguistics and advanced semantics.
Mrs Overall	Well, I had to do something while I was recovering from that transplant.
Babs	Yes, we were grateful to you for donating all that bone marrow to Miss Berta.
Mrs Overall	I hope she got it all right.
Babs	I'm afraid some of it had leaked out of the Jiffy bag.
Mrs Overall	Men!

Slight hiatus.

Babs	Yes, the doctors are very pleased with her.
Mrs Overall	I heard she may never play the gramophone again.
Babs	Oh, that sounds like the postman. That looks like an important letter.

Props boy tries to stuff large envelope through the letter box – it won't go – he pushes it through the side of the door.

I'll get it, Mrs O – oh, you're too quick for me – I can never lift a finger when you're around.

Mrs Overall sets off very slowly for the door.

Mrs Overall	*(pronouncing it correctly)* It's your decree nisi, Miss Babs.
Babs	*(pronouncing it the same way)* 'Nisi', Mrs O.
Mrs Overall	'Nisi'. I always get that word wrong.
Babs	I can't bear to look – have I got custody of the triplets?
Mrs Overall	I'm afraid not, Miss Babs, but you have won a weekend for two in the Peak District and a deep fat fryer.
Babs	Do you think those triplets were really mine, Mrs O? After all, I did only go into hospital to have my ears pierced.
Mrs Overall	Well, look at it this way – you can't break an omelette

without beating eggs. Eating eggs.

Babs sighs ruefully.

Music.

Film. Ext. day. Hospital. Berta comes out, sees a crawling mini-cab, hails it and gets in.

Int. Back of cab. Berta is actually saying something like 'I'll just pretend to be saying something'.

Berta   *(dubbed on later)* Acorn Antiques, please.

Scene Two. Dining Room. A dining table with chairs along one side only, to leave room for the cameras at the other side of the table. Babs, Clifford and Trixie sit facing the camera. Trixie dressed as a nun, loads of eye make-up etc. On cue, they all put down their spoons as if they've just finished their pudding.

Trixie   Oh Mummy, that was a truly delicious Prune Melba.
Babs   High praise indeed from a Mother Superior!
Trixie   Oh Mummy, you know I've been expelled from the
                 convent. I'm only wearing this old habit because I forgot
                 to collect my dry cleaning.
Clifford   Yes, why did you get expelled?
Trixie   *(off-hand)* Oh, I just broke a few things.
Clifford   Like what?
Trixie   Oh, just a few vows.
Babs   Listen!

Sound of black cab.

Clifford   *(very slowly)* It sounds like –

Babs	*(jumping in)* I think you're right.
Clifford	*(determined to finish his line)* A taxi.
Babs	Derek can't be back from the clinic this early.

Enter Berta with a carry-cot, tilted at a dangerous angle.

	Berta!
Berta	You may as well know, I've discharged myself.
Babs	Come and sit down, you're just in time for coffee.
	Clifford, run and fetch Mrs O.

Berta sits down.

She's in the scullery stuffing an aubergine. Trixie – show him the way.

Clifford leaves very slowly, Trixie can't get past him.

Now, I couldn't help noticing – what's in the carry-cot?

| Berta | See for yourself. |

Cut to library film of a baby in a different carry-cot.

| Babs | A baby! Where did that come from? And while we're on the subject – where's your eighty per cent lambswool eau-de-nil donkey jacket? |
| Berta | I, I . . . |

Mrs Overall appears in shot without having come through the door.

| Mrs Overall | Miss Berta! You've never gone and done one of your silly, silly swaps! |

Music.
Credits.

Berta	But that's enough about me, what's all this building work I saw as I came in?
Babs	I should have sent you a telemessage –
Mrs Overall	The fact is, Miss Berta, Acorn Antiques is re-opening as a health club and leisure centre.

Reaction from Berta. Screen goes blank.

Mrs Overall	*(Voice Over)* With sun beds! *(In own voice)* Why, why, why do I always forget those darn sun beds, anybody know?

Episode Ten

Scene One. The shop. Extras as before but now dressed in towelling dressing gowns with 'AA' on the back, and flippers. Babs is in her usual gear, with a sweatband round her wig.

Babs	Enjoy your swim – just leave your antiques in the cubicle – they'll be perfectly safe.

Extras nod and smile without speaking. Enter Berta from another door in top half of suit, tracksuit pants and court shoes.

	Berta! Feel better for your run?
Berta	I certainly do. After all, running does keep you fit and could be a considerable contributory factory in reducing heart disease. Where's Mrs O? It was only the thought of her macaroons that kept me going.
Babs	*(pressing buttons on new intercom)* Mrs Overall, coffee for two in reception, please. Now *(leaves button pressed down, strange female voice comes from it)*
Voice	– went all the way to Nottingham, all the way back.

Babs switches it off.

Babs	Now – there's something I've been meaning to –

Enter Derek and Trixie in judo gear. Trixie with lots of jewellery and high heels.

Babs	Ah! Derek and Trixie, how did you get on in the international judo competition?
Derek	We came third, Miss Babs. Tibet was first, then Manchesterford.
Babs	Well done. Now get along to Maintenance, Derek, please. A parcel's just arrived and we haven't a clue if it's a Henry Moore or part of the central heating.
Derek	Right away, Miss Babs *(doesn't move)*.
Babs	*(supposedly stopping him in the doorway)* Oh, Derek –
Derek	Yes, Miss Babs?
Babs	Oh, nothing, it doesn't matter.
Trixie	Mummy?
Babs	Yes, darling?
Trixie	Oh, nothing, it doesn't matter.
Berta	Mrs O is being a long time with those macaroons. I hope –
Babs	What?
Berta	Oh, nothing – it doesn't matter.

Enter Mrs Overall.

Babs	Mrs O, you have been a long time, I hope there's nothing wrong.
Mrs Overall	Why should there be anything wrong, Miss Babs?
Babs	No reason, it's just –
Mrs Overall	Except of course that –
Babs	That?
Berta	Go on.
Trixie	Yes?
Mrs Overall	Except that – oh, it's nothing, it doesn't matter.

Reaction from other three. Music.

Film. Usual street. Babs walking along, reaches a doctor's house, looks up at the name plate, checks it on the piece of paper she's carrying (cut in close-up of piece of paper held by hairy male hand), checks the name plate again, steels herself and goes in.

Scene Two. Sitting room. Babs, Berta (still with sweatbands) and Clifford (in tennis gear with tan make-up stopping just below the chin). Enter Mrs Overall in leotard and tights, and carrying tray.

Mrs Overall Here we are. A nice tray of decaffeinated coffee with low-fate milk and sugar-free sugar.

Babs Goodness, how healthy.

Mrs Overall Oh, I enjoyed myself.

Babs And how was the aerobics class?

Mrs Overall Oh, I enjoyed myself. The correct footwear, a supportive brassière to prevent chafing and plenty of individual attention from a qualified instructor.

Babs It sounds ideal *(suddenly looks worried)*.

Mrs Overall It was only the exercises I didn't take to.

Clifford Babs? You look pensive.

Babs No I'm not, I was just thinking.

Berta *(getting up with difficulty, wedged in the sofa)* Well, I think I'll go for a ten-mile bicycle ride.

Babs Well, don't forget your florescent clothing and protective headgear.

Berta I won't.

Babs And Berta –

Berta Ah – ha?

Babs Oh, nothing – it doesn't matter.

Exit Berta.

Look, you two, this isn't easy to say . . .

Mrs Overall I knew it – the mysterious man with the bins seen lurking by the binoculars – it's Trixie's twin cousin, isn't it, he won't rest until Acorn Antiques Leisure Centre and Sunbed Centre has been closed down.

Music.
Credits.

Babs *(The table is now covered in milk dripping everywhere.)* No, it's not that. I went to see our family doctor, Dr Wimley, today.

Mrs Overall Oh, Miss Babs, what did he say?

Clifford Yes, for heck's sake Babs, what did the doctor say?

Babs He said he was sorry about the noise but there were men outside digging up the pavement.

Episode Eleven

Scene One. Shop. Extras as before (no dressing gowns). Babs staring at letter. Enter Berta from the house.

Berta Is that the bill from the wholesalers?

Babs Yes, and its rather puzzling.

Berta Why, what does it say?

Babs See for yourself.

Babs breathes huge sigh and blows it off the table.

Berta *(trying to appear to read it and still stay in shot)* That's ridiculous. They've charged us for seven Laughing Cavaliers!

Babs It must be a misprint, I'm sure we only ordered four.

Enter Mrs Overall.

Mrs Overall   I know it's only a quarter to, but I've just this minute whipped my coconut buns out of the microwave. Miss Berta?

Berta   Well, you know me and coconut.

Mrs Overall   Not to worry. We got it all out of the carpet last time. How's the baby, Miss Berta? Still breastfeeding?

Berta   Well, I know I should be passing on my immunities, but with a bra-slip and a jersey two-piece it's just not on.

Babs   Clifford should have been here by now.

Clifford can be seen through the window of the shop, laughing animatedly, talking to a stage-hand.

Mrs Overall   He's been looking very strange these past few days. I hope he hasn't done anything silly.

Babs   Anything silly?

Berta   Like what?

Mrs Overall   Like putting on a false nose and learning the banjulele.

Berta   No, it's all right, I can hear his car.

Babs   Yes, thank heavens he has such a distinctive horn.

Clifford stubs out his fag on the set, and acting ponderously as before, comes into the shop.

Clifford! What's wrong, you're as white as a sheet! *(He's as brown as ever.)*

Clifford   I have something to tell you, Babs.

Berta   Shall I go?

Clifford   No, stay. And please come back, Mrs O. *(She hasn't moved but does so on his line.)* What I have to say concerns everybody.

Sits down heavily on a small ornate table, the leg crunches and he slips sideways a few inches.

Film. Street. Derek pacing up and down outside the shop door. He comes to a decision and walks away.

Scene Two. Sitting Room. Mrs Overall standing. Clifford sitting.

Mrs Overall Come on, Mr Clifford – while Miss Babs and Miss Berta are sellotaping that bit back onto Michelangelo's 'David', why don't you tell me all about it?

Clifford The fact is, Mrs O, my life seems completely grey, bleak and pointless.

Mrs Overall Yes well, sometimes that's God's way of getting you to enjoy 'Gardener's World'.

Clifford stands up suddenly, catching the boom operator unawares, hits his head on it, and collapses in pain, moaning. Mrs Overall is oblivious to all this.

Mrs Overall You see, you're smiling, things can't be all that bad, out with it!

Clifford *(in pain)* Bloody Norah. Oh, blimey.

Mrs Overall Oh, you're not! Mr Clifford, what shocking news!

Enter Babs and Berta.

Well, I finally winkled it out of him, Miss Babs, and it took some winkling.

Babs Don't say any more, Mrs O. The baby alarm was on in the antiques packing department, and Berta and I heard the whole darn thing!

Music.
Credits.

Enter Derek in street clothes, nearly the same as in the film. Clifford has left the set.

Babs Yes, come in Derek, we all know your sordid little secret. Why don't you and Clifford have a session right here and now?

Derek	That's what I came to tell your Mr Clifford. The accordion and the banjulele – they've disappeared into thin air!

Reaction from Clifford's chair.

Episode Twelve

Scene One. The sitting room. Berta ironing a shirt. Clifford, Trixie and Derek are all jammed on the sofa.

Berta	So you and Derek weren't having an affair after all?
Trixie	Oh, no. He was just lying on top of me to get the creases out of my negligée.
Berta	I knew there must be a perfectly reasonable explanation.
Trixie	*(struggling up from the sofa)* Anyway, I have to get back to the convent.
Berta	The convent? Why?
Trixie	I forgot my teapot.
Derek	I'll give you a lift.
Trixie	Well, all right, but don't crash through a grocer's window this time. Those tinned pears really hurt me. Bye!

Exit Derek and Trixie.

Berta	Bye! *(having completely mangled the shirt).*
Berta	There, that looks a bit better.
Clifford	Perfect. Berta – I've been meaning to –
Berta	Just unplug the iron for me, could you?
Clifford	A pleasure *(he bends to do so).*
Berta	Only don't touch it with your bare hands because . . .
Clifford	Argggh!
Berta	Because . . . it's faulty . . .

Enter Mrs Overall with a tray.

Mrs Overall Whatever was that heartrending scream, Miss Berta? I thought somebody was being electrocuted.
Berta Look!
Mrs Overall Oh, my good golliwog!

She drops the tray on Clifford's foot.

Clifford Ow!
Berta Is he – dead?
Mrs Overall Well, put it this way, Miss Berta, I needn't have bothered rinsing out the extra mug.
Berta No, Clifford will never touch your macaroons again!

Enter Babs.

Babs What was that terrible noise? It sounded like a tray of coffee being dropped on someone who's just been electrocuted.
Mrs Overall
Berta *(nearly together)* Look!
Babs He's dead. *(Bursts into tears.)*
Mrs Overall Crying won't bring him back, Miss Babs.
Babs *(cheering up)* No, that's true.
Mrs Overall Why don't we all have a mug of my delicious home-made sherry and a couple of sausage dumplings?
Babs Yes, Mrs O, why don't we?

They all laugh. Music.

Film. Street. Derek and Trixie bring out from the back of the Acorn Antiques van a large cardboard carton labelled 'Venus de Milo. Fragile. This way up. Use no Hooks' etc. They take it into the shop.

Scene Two. The shop. Extras leaving as usual, Babs on the phone.

Babs   *(waving goodbye to extras)* Ah oui, bien sûr, j'aime beaucoup le World Cup, aussi. Naturellement. Au revoir.

Babs puts the phone down. Derek and Trixie come in with carton, now upside down. Next dialogue at high speed.

Derek   We've brought the 'Venus de Milo', Miss Babs.
Trixie   And we want to say goodbye.
Babs   Goodbye? But why?
Derek   We're going away.
Babs   Away? Where?
Trixie   Together.
Babs   Together? When?
Derek   We're going overland to Morocco.
Babs   You're going overland to Morocco? Why?

Enter Berta from street.

Berta   What's wrong, Babs?
Babs   It's Derek and Trixie; they're going away, travelling overland to Morocco, together.
Berta   Derek and Trixie are overland travelling away to Morocco, together. But why?
Trixie   Everyone says you can get really nice jumpsuits. Bye!

Trixie and Derek leave.

Babs   Right – back to business – these antiques.

Babs draws Berta away to one side as the focus of the scene changes to Mrs Overall, who enters stealthily from the street and tiptoes past them. We are not supposed to hear their

dialogue but the mike is in the wrong place.

Babs   I'll just go blah blah blah blah.

Berta   And I'll nod back blah blah blah blah . . .

Babs   Give the blithering old nuisance time to get to the table. Chippendale.

Berta   Mahogany.

Babs   Da da de dum. Right. Mrs O! We never heard you come in. What happened to the body?

Mrs Overall   Mr Clifford? He's gone nice and stiff, so I've propped him up by the ironing board.

Babs   How lovely.

Mrs Overall   Well he was that tall, there was no room to hoover.

Berta   Mmm, what's that delicious smell?

Mrs Overall   That must be my macaroons. I've had them on a low light since Wednesday.

Berta   I'll get them.

Exit Berta.

Mrs Overall   Slice them finely, or someone might choke to death . . . I don't think she heard me. *(Pulls face to indicate sudden worry.)*

Babs   What's wrong, Mrs O?

Mrs Overall   The tea-leaves in my cup this morning, something's wrong somewhere.

Babs   Why?

Mrs Overall   It was a cup of Horlicks.

Babs   It's strange to think of Clifford lying in the sitting room, all alone.

Clifford seen in outdoor clothes crossing the back of the set with a bag, waving goodbye to someone unseen, miming 'Let's have a drink', etc.

Mrs Overall   Not to worry. When Mr Overall (no relation) was dying, he said, 'Well, Boadicea, I shall never have to play

	another game of Travel Scrabble.'
Babs	Why did he call you Boadicea?
Mrs Overall	He was barmy, Miss Babs.

Berta comes in with the tray.

Berta	Your macaroons smell delicious.
Babs	Yes, Mrs O, you sample the first one.
Mrs Overall	Well, I will, but just in case anything should happen when I bite into it *(music)* I just want to say what I feel for Acorn Antiques and the folk who work there. I'm only a simple woman, I haven't any 'O' levels or life-saving certificates, I've never been abroad or fully participated in a Summit Conference, but I have feelings . . .

Babs and Berta gradually stop acting and get bored.

> . . . and what I feel for Acorn Antiques and you Miss Babs and you Miss Berta *(turns macaroon over, it has a few scribbled lines pasted on it)* is nothing more or less than plain simple *(squints at macaroon)* cove – love.

She bites into it, chokes to death, and carefully lowers herself to the floor, avoiding the furniture and pulling down her skirt.

Babs	She's choking on her own macaroon. Quick, get Dr Wimley, the family doctor!
Berta	I can't, he's being blackmailed in the Sudan.
Babs	Oh, darn. Well, quite frankly Berta, as far as Mrs O is concerned, it's far too late.

Abrupt change from mood music to theme music.
Credits.
Cut back to Babs and Berta in tears crouched uncomfortably by Mrs Overall.

| **Babs** | Mrs Overall – that macaroon you just choked on – I'm going to send the recipe to the *Weekly News*. |

Mrs Overall Oh, I am pleased.

She dies. Pause.

(In own voice) Are we off? I thought that went quite well, didn't you?

Voice Off Still on air!

She dies again reluctantly.

THE END

THE MAKING OF
Acorn Antiques

The Making of Acorn Antiques

*Int. Office. Day. Opening sequence of 'Acorn Antiques' –
entirely as usual. Camera pulls back – we are watching a TV
screen in the 'Acorn Antiques' production office. Paul Heiney is
sitting on a desk watching it. He switches it off with his remote
control and swivels to camera.*

Paul   How many people tune in to hear that oh-so-familiar
music every evening? About fifty-four. But what goes on
behind the scenes? What *don't* the public see? *(He runs the
sentence through again in his head, then carries on.)*

Walks over to a door marked 'Script Conference In Progress'

Let's find out what exactly does or doesn't go into the
making of 'Acorn Antiques'.

CAPTION 'THE MAKING OF "ACORN ANTIQUES"'

Paul taps on the door.

Marion   *(out of vision)* Get out!

---

*Conference room. Day. Marion Clune, at the head of the table,
is checking through that week's scripts, talking into a phone
jammed into her neck and checking a wallplan behind her, all
at the same time. Round the table are Simon, the weedy
director, and a few writers including Roberts and Watkins.*

Paul   *(out of vision)* It's seven o'clock on Monday morning and
Marion Clune, 'Acorn Antiques'' much feared executive
producer, is knocking the week's scripts into shape.
Marion   *(tossing the scripts back like homework)* Blake, Thursday's
not bad, Roberts, Monday's script – not totally bananas

	about the AIDS story – would Mrs Overall really know what a condom is?
Simon	*(eagerly)* She could call it a 'Comdon'.
Marion	*(seriously)* Yes, that's very funny, we'll use it. No, this AIDS idea has been an itsy bit overplayed – let's box a wee bit dangerous – I'm talking off the top of my hairdo now – let's really go for it – earwax – I've never seen it tackled – it's an issue, it's health – suppose Berta gets earwax – no – she finds a syringe.
Roberts	Could I just throw something in here, Marion?
Marion	Feel free, mucho libre –
Roberts	I think perhaps AIDS has more potential, dramatically, than earwax.
Marion	*(not even looking up)* Right, you're fired. Don't talk to the press if you like having kneecaps *(tossing another script back as Roberts leaves, stunned)*. Tuesday's script, very good Watkins – funny way to spell 'Acorn'. Friday's . . .

Ext. Church hall. Day.

Paul	And those very scripts end up here, where the actors and director sweat to produce the magic that *is* 'Acorn Antiques'.

He goes inside.

Church hall. The floor is marked up. A few odd pieces of furniture. Thermoses in a corner where Albert and Michaela are sitting. Far away from them sits Mrs Overall in lovely tailored slacks. Clifford sits alone, embroidering a tray cloth. In the middle of rehearsing stand Babs in jaunty casuals and unfamiliar hairdo and Derek resplendent in an off-the-shoulder overcoat and toupé. Simon watches intently, making squares of his fingers to represent the camera lens.

Babs	*(mumbling to herself)* Put the phone down. Down it goes, turn to Derek . . . Simon? Yes?
Derek	And I'll look sort of questioningly at you.
Babs	*(off-hand)* Will you? So turn to Derek. 'That was the Immigration Authority, Derek.'

He gasps.

	Are you going to do that, because I'll leave a gap.
Derek	No, it was my tooth again.
Babs	Poor you. 'Immigration Authority, Derek. It's not good news, I'm afraid.'
Derek	Miss Babs?
Babs	Can't we cut that 'Miss Babs'? It's Bab Bab Bab every two minutes. Anyone mind? Simon? No? OK. 'Good news, I'm afraid. You're being repatriated, you've to catch the first train to Kirkcudbright tomorrow morning.'
Derek	It's Kirkcudbright.
Babs	I know that – Babs wouldn't. Simon? Agreed?
Derek	Then I'll look – because he's quite stunned by this news, isn't he?
Babs	No idea.
Derek	Then I'll turn and go *(starts to do it very slowly and dramatically)*.
Babs	*(walking off the set)* The camera's on me there anyway, isn't it? Simon? Yes? Tea break? Simon? Yes? Black coffee please, Albert!

Calls from everyone else for tea and coffee.
Berta dashes in.

Berta	Hello!

They all gather round concernedly, cries of 'Darling!' 'How is everything?', etc.

Mrs Overall	Oh darling, how did you get on?
Babs	Oh yes darling, any luck?
Berta	Not bad *(waves carrier bag)*. No éclairs, but a lot of those nice long doughnuts.

Cries of 'well done', 'how marvellous', etc.

Same. Paul, Mrs Overall and Kenny sitting a little way off from the others.

Paul	Are you like the part you play? Are you in fact Mrs Overall?
Mrs Overall	I think Bo and I are rather alike, Paul, yes . . .
Paul	Bo?
Mrs Overall	Boadicea. We're both rather gutsy ladies, very determined, strong moral sense, we've both had rather difficult lives, a certain amount of personal loss . . . *(She loses her thread as she dwells on this.)*
Derek	They're both very warm and very giving.
Mrs Overall	*(patting his hand)* Bless you for that, my darling. And of course I'm rather younger and I hope rather more attractive!

They all laugh.

Paul	*(laughing)* So the famous lumpy tights and, er, varicose veins are just something that goes on with the make-up?
Mrs Overall	*(after nasty silence)* Have you got the crossword, Kenny my darling?

Same. Clifford and Paul

Paul	Are you all one big happy family? Do you all get on well?
Clifford	*(thinks)* I should say, on the whole, no.

Same. Mrs Overall, Derek and Paul.

Paul	There's been rather a lot made in the Press of a feud between you and certain younger members of the cast – any truth in that?
Mrs Overall	*(shrugging enigmatically)* Dear Paul, I'm a huge, huge star – this is the price I pay. Look how the Press treated poor Yorky.
Derek	Fergie.
Mrs Overall	Fergie.

Ext. The location shop front and street. Day.

*Marion and Simon in earnest conversation as the camera is
being set up for a shot of Mrs Overall leaving the shop with a
letter. Paul is hanging around, not liking to interrupt.*

Paul	*(out of vision)* Thursday is set aside for outside filming, and here on the 'Acorn Antiques' lot a tricky shot is being discussed.
Marion	So Mrs Overall comes out, takes out the letter, posts it, goes back in. Bueno. Let's shoot it.
Simon	Except we haven't got the letter box.
Paul	Ah – so –
Marion	*(furious)* Mickey! Here! Now! *(The props boy Mickey runs up.)*
Mickey	Yes, Miss Clune?
Marion	*(slapping him on each side of the head in turn)* You don't – chew – gum. *(Holding hand out)* Take it out. Give it to me. You're fired. What say, Simon?
Simon	*(agitated)* No letter box, she can't post the letter.
Marion	No problem. Nila problemo. Slip in a line 'Oh Miss Babs the letter box has been stolen by international terrorists, what a palaver . . .'

*Mrs Overall with a fur coat over her costume, supported by
Derek, totters up.*

Simon	What, and pick that up in another story later?
Marion	No *(concerned)*. How are they, Bo?
Mrs Overall	They're fine, I'm fine. Kenny – if you could hover with my Veganin?
Kenny	*(taking her coat)* I'll be here.
Paul	Is there some sort of problem –
Marion	*(back to business)* Small change, Bo – the letter box has been stolen –
Mrs Overall	So I come out –
Marion	Come out –
Mrs Overall	Walk walk walk to the pillar box –
Marion	Blimey oh fiddledebob – no pillar box.
Mrs Overall	React react react.
Marion	That's it.
Simon	Oh fantastic, it's here!

Man in anorak dumps down pillar box.

Marion	Right – back to plan A – there is now a pillar box.
Mrs Overall	Oh, there is a pillar box. First there's no pillar box, then one appears. What next, no pavement, no shop? *(She notices Paul and the film crew.)* Sorry, do you mind – this is rather a tricky manoeuvre – rather fussing to be filming as one's working.
Paul	OK. Cut it.

Make-up room. Babs and Berta larding it on. Clifford being made up by girl, Derek hanging round chatting to him.

Paul	*(out of vision)* It's Friday, just time for a quick make-up check before the cameras finally roll.
Girl	I thought perhaps as Mr Clifford has been in prison for a year, he perhaps would be quite pasty, so I thought I'd use this instead of the Cool Copper.
Clifford	No, I'll stick with the usual, I think.
Paul	So where will I find Mrs Overall?
Babs	In her dressing room, I expect.
Derek	*(out of vision)* I said 'Excuse me – I had leather shorts before George Formby had a ukulele' –
Paul	So you've all got a dressing room to relax in, have you?
Berta	No, not all of us.

Mrs Overall's cosy dressing room. The room is full of flowers, cards, photos of Russell Grant, Derek and Mrs Overall's mother, stuffed toys etc.

Paul	And these are all presents?
Mrs Overall	People are so so so kind. I'm just a jobbing actress, who scraped to put herself through the RADA and yet somehow I've captured the hearts of the nation – it's almost frightening.
Paul	*(sniffing at fancy jar)* And what's this?
Mrs Overall	It's a haemorrhoid preparation to be brutally frank, Paul *(winces as she takes it from him).*

Studio, the usual set. Albert and Michaela position themselves by their antique. Babs, Berta and Clifford sort themselves out by the desk.

Paul   *(out of vision)* This is it. This is the moment when all that hard work pays off. As the actors stand by on the studio floor . . .

Int. Gallery. Day. Marion, Simon and batty PA.

Paul   *(out of vision)* . . . Marion and Simon get ready to record episode 1,573 of 'Acorn Antiques'.

Marion   *(into mike)* OK, running up recording. You've done a marvellous week's work – relax, enjoy it, but above all – don't touch the antiques – I want them back in my lounge in one piece. Stand by.

Simon   Cue titles.

Opening sequence comes up on monitors.

Side of set. Mrs Overall with Paul, waiting to enter with tray.

Paul   How are you feeling?

Mrs Overall   I won't talk, Paul my darling, I just have to gather myself in, focus . . . 'be' . . .

Gallery (as before).

Simon   Cue Albert and Michaela.

PA   Coming to 2. No . . . 3. No, it *was* 2. Now coming to 3. Oh . . .

Simon   And in on Babs!

Babs   *(on monitor)* I've had a most peculiar letter . . .

Marion   Good and close camera 2. Love those nostrils.

Side of set (as before).

Mrs Overall   *(in full flow)* And Princess Margaret is so like me, give,

give, give *(hands Paul the tray)*. Do you mind, I did
promise the specialist – well –

Gallery (as before).

Berta   *(on monitor)* I don't know about you Clifford, but I could
          jolly well do with a nice cup of tea and a chocolate bhaji.
Babs   So could jolly well I.
Marion   *(over Babs's line)* Nice nod to the Asians there.
PA   Coming to 3. Oh, what page are we on now?
Simon   Stand by, Mrs Overall, steady on the doorway 3.

Side of set (as before).

Mrs Overall I said – for you Lord Delfont –

Assistant Floor Manager runs up frantically waving.

I'm talking Sally – for you, Lord Delfont it will be a
pleasure and an honour.

*Gallery (as before). Monitor: Babs, Clifford and Berta wait
silently.*

Simon   Where is she? Cue her!
Marion   She'll be there, be calm, be calm. *(Screaming)* COME
          ON!

Side of set (as before).

AFM   You're on!
Mrs Overall I'm aware of that Sally, after thirty years in the business.

Goes on, leaving Paul with the tray.

Gallery (as before).

Simon   No tray! Where's the bloody tray?
Marion   We'll cope.

Simon	It's mentioned!
Marion	Mentioned?

Cut to close-up of monitor.

Babs	Mrs Overall, we could smell your bhajis a mile away!
Berta	And do I spy a new tray?

Silence.

Marion	She'll get us out of it, come on Bo. Improvise!

Back to monitor.

Mrs Overall	Yes, I just had to bring it in and show you. Take it, isn't it light?
Babs	*(miming)* Mmm, and such a lovely shade of mauve. Look, Clifford!
Clifford	It's magnificent.
Simon	*(overlapping Babs's line)* Shall we cut? Go back?
Marion	No, we professionals notice these things, but Joe Public never clocks a darn thing.

She sits happily watching the monitor as Paul appears in the doorway with the tray.

Still Barmy

Spaghetti

Lunchtime in a small Italian restaurant. Philippa and Faith drinking wine.

Philippa Cheers.

Faith Cheers. How's things?

Philippa Oh, its been a terrible week. Monday I thought I was having an early menopause.

Faith And were you?

Philippa No, the dog had been beggaring about with the thermostat.

Faith I didn't know you had a dog.

Philippa It's my mother's. She's in Marbella for the winter. Twelve pounds a week all in.

Faith That's very cheap.

Philippa She's sharing a room with two dustmen.

Faith Does she like Spain?

Philippa She likes the majesty and grandeur of the landscape, but she's not keen on the bacon.

Faith What sort of dog is it?

Philippa Oh, performing. Rolls round the kitchen on a beach ball *(is interrupted by arrival of cheeky Italian waiter who serves two pasta dishes)*. Thank you.

Waiter Pasta – bit fattening, hey? Something to grab hold of . . . nice one *(They half-smile, he leaves.)*

Philippa They're all like that here. Jamming their groins into your tortellini. Then on Tuesday, Nick left home.

Faith What, for good?

Philippa He's taken the toolshed.

Faith I thought you were so well-suited.

Philippa We were – especially physically. Every time I gave him the old come hither, he came hither.

Faith You were quite experimental, weren't you?

Philippa Oh yes, outdoors; three in a bed –

Faith With the man next door?

Philippa I don't recommend it. They got on to politics and I ended up watching 'Take the High Road' with the sound off.

Waiter in.

Waiter Parmesan?
Philippa Thank you.
Faith Thank you.
Waiter Yum, yum, very nice, very cheesy.

Makes kissing noises and leaves.

Philippa We should have gone to the Snacketeria. One thing about self-service is no one tries to arouse your sexuality. No, Nick, apparently, is in love with someone else.
Faith How long's that been going on?
Philippa Must be yonks, because he told me 'their tune' was 'Chirpy Chirpy Cheep Cheep'.
Faith Who is it?
Philippa You know I mentioned a very small neighbour of mine – buys children's clothes and spends the VAT on tequila?
Faith Mmm.
Philippa It's her. I wondered why he'd had that cat-flap widened.

Waiter in with huge pepper mill.

Waiter Pepper, ladies? Make you nice and hot.
Both Thank you.
Waiter Nice big one, eh? I know what you ladies like *(leaves)*.
Philippa Thank heavens the sausage was off. So I'm totally disillusioned. No more sex, I'm going to become a nun.
Faith I thought you had to be able to play billiards.
Philippa Oh no, that's all changed. I'm joining a convent in Smethwick on Friday. I have to take one small suitcase and a jigsaw.
Faith What's the habit like?
Philippa Hot pants.
Faith They're very outdated.
Philippa Well, you have to make some sacrifices.
Faith Won't you miss the physical side of life?
Philippa No, Faith, because I'm basically a very cerebral and spiritual

person – I don't go round panting for bodily intimacy like a misguided poodle.

Waiter nuzzles up to Philippa.

Waiter   You like to come and be very naughty with me in the staff washroom? Lots of sexy fun with nice big Italian boy?

Philippa *(hesitating slightly)* Oh, go on then. Faith?

Faith   Just a black coffee, thank you.

Medical School

*An interview room. Two men and a woman behind a table.
Paralytically nervous girl in suit sitting down. All the
interviewers are completely non-committal throughout.*

First man Sit down, er, Sarah.
Sarah Thank you.
First man It's only an interview, we're not going to eat you.
Sarah Ha ha ha.
First man I see you're taking Biology, Physics, Chemistry and English, all good A levels for medical school. How do you think you're going to do?
Sarah Well, I might get an A for physics, I might get an A, two Bs and a C for biology or I might get a B for physics, what I get very much depends . . .
First man Thank you.
Second man I see you're doing the Duke of Edinburgh's Award Scheme – do you think that's character-building?
Sarah Yes, I think it builds character, it is character building, yes, it is a character building thing, yes.
Second man In what way does it build character, do you think?
Sarah In what way – I think in the way that – just the way you'd expect, really.
Second man Thank you.
First man Sarah – do you think there's any link between environment and disease?
Sarah Do you mean *the* environment?
First man Living conditions – do you think living conditions can affect health?
Sarah Yes, I think they probably can.
First man In what way?
Sarah If you shared a bedroom with someone who had measles then you might get measles, or if you were very rich and had very thick carpets you might trip and break your

	ankle, it would affect you in that way.
First man	What about if you were very poor?
Sarah	If you were very poor, then you wouldn't have that kind of carpet.
First man	Do you think poor housing would have an adverse effect on health?
Sarah	Yes, I think it would have an adverse effect on health because, because it would affect people's health adversely.
First man	Thank you.
Woman	Sarah – do you think there's a gap between the media's portrayal of doctors and doctors in real life?
Sarah	Yes I think there is a gap because the doctor in East Enders has bushy eyebrows and it might make people think that if you're a doctor you have to have bushy eyebrows and you might not have bushy eyebrows but you might want to be a doctor, and that's not really fair . . .
Woman	Thank you.
First man	What do you think about the National Health Service?
Sarah	In what way, 'think'?
First man	Do you think it's crumbling, or doing very well, or . . .
Sarah	I think that probably that parts of it are crumbling, and parts of it are doing very well, I think you have to look at both sides.
First man	Go on.
Sarah	Of course some people say well oh let's close casualty departments and spend the money on nuclear weapons but I think you have to sit back and say if there is a nuclear war then we'll need casualty departments.
Second man	You don't think in a nuclear war we'll all be annihilated?
Sarah	No.
Woman	What qualities do you think you'll bring to the medical profession? *(Pause.)* Are you particularly warm, or compassionate?
Sarah	I'm quite tidy.
Woman	Thank you.
First man	What was the last book you read, Sarah?
Sarah	*Othello.* It's a book by William Shakespeare of the Royal Shakespeare Company. I've got the book, and I've got it on little cards as well.

First man	What do you think is the main theme of *Othello*?
Sarah	I don't think it's got one, really. It's just various people talking, and sometimes they do things in brackets.
First man	And do you think Othello was ill –
Sarah	*(quickly)* No.
First man	To act in the way he did – was he suffering from anything, when he discovered Desdemona's handkerchief?
Sarah	I think he might have been suffering from a cold.
First man	Right Sarah, thank you very much indeed.

Sarah goes out. They write.

	I thought she was jolly good, didn't you?
Woman	Excellent.
Second man	Very astute.
First man	Unconditional offer?
Woman	Absolutely.
Second man	Definitely.

He didn't: One

Bus stop. Kelly-Marie Tunstall and her pal.

Kelly   So he walked over, right, big 'I am' and he had tattoos up his arms right, an anchor here and a microwave here.

Pal   He didn't.

Kelly	He did. He said do you want a drink or do you want a kick up the bum with an open-toed sandal. I said get you Eamonn Andrews.
Pal	You didn't.
Kelly	I did. I said I'll have a pint of babycham, some pork scratchings and a yellow cherry and if I'm not here when you get back I'll be in t' toilet putting hide and heal on my love bites.
Pal	You didn't.
Kelly	I did. So I come out of toilets, right, and he says hey scallop face your skirt's all caught up in your knickers at back, I said I pity you do you know why, he says why, I says 'cos it happens to be the latest fashion, I read it in a book, he says what book, I said Vogue that's what book, he said oh likely likely when do you read Vogue, I said when I'm in the hospital having exploratory surgery that's when. So he said oh.
Pal	He didn't.
Kelly	He did. And he sits there, right, picking the quiz off his beer-mat, and he says what were they exploring for, I said well it wasn't the Left Bank of the blinking Limpopo.
Pal	You didn't.
Kelly	I did. I said if you must know Magnus Magnusson I was rushed in last Wednesday when I swallowed the upholstery attachment of an Electrolux 567. He said how did you do that, I said I were hoovering a pelmet with my mouth open. Like that.
Pal	You weren't.
Kelly	I was. He said was it a long operation, I said it was a bit longer than normal because while they were stitching me I said could they put a new zip in my drainpipes.
Pal	You didn't.
Kelly	I did. Anyway, he stands up and he says do you want to come for a Chinese or do you want a clip round the ear with a wrestler's braces? I said I'll come for a Chinese because I've had a clip round the ear with a wrestler's braces and there's nowt to it.
Pal	You didn't.
Kelly	I did. He fell about laughing. Like this. I could see all cheese and onion crisps in his fillings.
Pal	You couldn't.

Kelly	I could. So we sit down and he says right I'm bloke I'm ordering, I says haven't you ever heard of Women's Lib he says no, I said oh. Anyway, we get t'end of meal, right, he's having a crack at burping and I'm chasing a lychee round a saucer, he says can I walk you home?
Pal	He didn't.
Kelly	He did. I said what's brought this on, bird bath? I said you needn't get any funny ideas because my mum and dad'll be up, I don't fancy you, and the surgeon says I can't joggle about for a fortnight.
Pal	He didn't.
Kelly	Who?
Pal	Surgeon.
Kelly	He did. So I said you can walk me home, but you're not pressing me up against the doorbell. So he puts down his banana fritter, he says Kelly-Marie Tunstall, just because I have tattoos and a hairy navel button does not mean I do not have the instincts of an English gentleman. Please believe me when I say I will be happy to escort you to your abode of residence, asking nothing in return but the chance of seeing you again.
Pal	He didn't.
Kelly	No, he didn't. He caught his bus and I had to pay for my own lychees.

Tattoo Parlour

*Small shop, a few sample designs on the wall, and electric
equipment. Two young slightly drunk sailors come in, ring the bell
for service and stand shoving each other and laughing. Enter nice
cosy woman.*

Woman   Can I help you, boys?
Eric   Isn't there a feller?
Woman   Mr Armstrong's having a lie down, I'm afraid. I'd rather not wake him. He's just done flags of all nations on a twelve-stone Wren.
Eric   Shall we go, Paul?
Woman   I'm a qualified tattooist as well as my husband. That's how we met. I had the shop next door, and he used to pop over if I needed an extra hand with a tricky buttock.
Paul   There's another shop up the road, isn't there?
Woman   Harry Abraham's? You should be all right there, they do have marvellous antibiotics these days, don't they?
Paul   How do you mean?
Woman   Apart from which he bolts his food.
Eric   Eh?
Woman   One hiccup halfway through the execution of a naked woman, and you're going through life with a bicep full of hermaphrodite.
Eric   OK, well we'll stay here then, shall we?
Woman   Lovely, right. Have a seat. What designs had you in mind?
Eric   Don't know – we only came in because we couldn't get into 'Bambi'.
Paul   What about a name? My girlfriend's name.
Woman   What is her name, dear?
Paul   Pat.
Woman   Not much to get your teeth into there. Hardly worth plugging the needle in for. I should leave that till you meet a girl who'll pay for a good bit of scrolling.

Eric	My girl at home's called Suzannah Margaret Mary.
Woman	Is it a steady relationship?
Paul	Not really.
Woman	You see, by the time I was up to the double 'n' you could have split up. Then you're either scouting round for another Suzannah Margaret Mary, or you find a girl with another name altogether who's broadminded, illiterate or never reads in bed. No, if you're stuck on having a name, boys, have something that can't cause embarrassment in later life, like 'Mother' or 'Miriam Stoppard'.
Eric	No . . .
Paul	What about an anchor and 'HMS Indestructible'? On my arm.
Woman	Yes, but what happens when you leave the Navy? It's going to look very incongruous if you go into the antiques business and have to roll your sleeves up to manoeuvre a Chesterfield.
Paul	I never thought of that.
Woman	This is what I'm here for – we don't want you to roll in here drunk and wake up the next morning covered in inappropriate remarks.
Eric	Hey – daggers! A pointed dagger, and it's dripping blood – like in three drops.
Woman	Not very cheerful, a dagger. If you're set on dripping, how about a leaky teapot?
Eric	No . . .
Paul	Hey – a panther! No, a cheetah – pouncing – right across my back – like that! *(Points to picture.)*
Woman	Stand up. Mmm. You've not really got the breadth of back for a fully successful cheetah. Have to be something a bit smaller. How about a Chihuahua?
Paul	Chihuahuas don't pounce.
Woman	They do if you tread on them.
Eric	*(ripping his shirt off and posing)* I've got a big back – I could have a cheetah.
Woman	Yes, but you see, dear, by the time I'd woven its paws in and out of your acne, it wouldn't be pouncing so much as waving.
Paul	*(laughing)* Tell her what you said to me on the way in.
Eric	What?
Paul	You know!
Eric	I didn't know it were a woman then, did I?

Woman	Oh, I've seen it all before dear – think of me as an usherette.
Paul	He said he wanted a Ferrari on his – thingy.
Woman	Well I'm happy to do that, though you must understand in moments of excitement it will distort. And if you're posted to a cold climate it may tend to look more like a Reliant Robin. *(They sit dejected.)* Look, why not have one of our set pieces? *(Demonstrating on one of them:)* The Parthenon across here, rambling roses to the elbow, two naked women either side of the spinal column, Caucasian or Oriental depending on what ink there is in the stockroom, a map of the London underground down each leg, finishing across here with an illustrated recipe for Baked Alaska.
Paul	That's sounds great, doesn't it, Eric? How much is that?
Woman	Eight colours and a no-fade warranty – 350 pounds.
Eric	We can't afford it.
Woman	Never mind boys, how much money have you got?

They sift through their pockets.

Paul	We spent a lot on booze, didn't we?
Eric	*(sheepishly)* About four quid.
Woman	And you want a tattoo for that?
Eric	Yes.
Woman	OK, Boys. *(Slapping a transfer on the back of his hand)* Lick that.

Partly Political Broadcast

Caption: 'Jean and Barbara'.

Barbara	Just to say if Jean and I are elected, we're obviously going to do our best to serve the constituency. I'm going to serve it Monday through Wednesday.
Jean	And I'll do Thursday through Saturday.
Barbara	And we'll do alternative Sundays, because I like to worship on that day.
Jean	And I like to have a good go at the kitchen cupboards.
Barbara	We both know this area pretty well, don't we.
Jean	Yes, in fact we can remember when the Old Malthouse Arts Centre used to be a Bingo Hall.
Barbara	That's right, and, and the Co-op used to do coffee and a little bun-ny-type snack for forty pence, do you remember?
Jean	Yes, because that's where you knocked into that stand of ovenproof tableware with your wonky buggy.
Barbara	And we said pity it wasn't buggy-proof! *(Laughs.)* Anyway. We're both quite political, aren't we?
Jean	Reasonably political. I was originally Liberal, and still think David Steel has a lot of credibility, popping up to the Borders every weekend to chop logs.
Barbara	And I was a Conservative, but looking back I think I was swayed by their rhetoric. And of course their garden parties had the best bran tubs.
Jean	You had those secateurs for years, didn't you?
Barbara	But we've both broken away, haven't we? Rather like Shirley Williams, whom we both admire, on the whole.
Jean	We feel she needs a little updating, eyeshadow-wise, but –
Barbara	And we've formed a new political party.
Jean	It's just called the Jean and Barbara Political Party.
Barbara	It's got its own colour.

Jean	The mainstream parties seem to have left the field clear as far as pastels are concerned.
Barbara	So we plumped for taupe.
Jean	Mushroom.
Barbara	Can we just say we've always been very active in local politics, haven't we?
Jean	Oh yes, I wrote to the papers and said now the dustmen didn't have to hump the actual bins, should we still tip?
Barbara	And we both boycotted a restaurant once where there was a strike.
Jean	That's right. The waiters were holding placards up outside asking you not to go in.
Barbara	So we didn't.
Jean	We never went in anyway.
Barbara	No, but we were still making a firm political stance. In fact we popped back after we'd done our shopping and boycotted it again, didn't we?
Jean	But we definitely know what people in this area want, don't we? Have you got our manifesto, Ba?
Barbara	*(rooting in handbag)* No, I think I used it to jam my quarterlight.
Jean	Well, anyway. It was – libraries. More Large Print novels, especially Jackie Collins.
Barbara	That's for my grandad. He likes smut and he can't focus.
Jean	More ramps. Ramp access – very very important for the wheelchair-bound.
Barbara	And for the able-bodied, it's a lovely tone-up for the calves and thighs *(slapping them)*.
Jean	Proper sugar bowls on each table at The Swiss Cottage, not packets by the till.
Barbara	Free dental treatment for old and sundry alike.
Jean	Especially the woman on the pastry counter at Lewis's because she's just upsetting, I won't go in.
Barbara	We want an increase in Family Income Supplement; we want a more frequent bus service.
Jean	And we want a much bigger hut at the Sauna Centre, it's nose to nipple in there.
Barbara	Mixed Wednesdays you have to beat them with twigs to get them to come out! But seriously . . .
Jean	Yes. *(Pause.)* Well, that's about it. I'd better go, Ba, I'm

doing something out of a book with sweetbreads.

They gather up their things.

Barbara	Anyway, so vote for us if you feel like it next Thursday.
Jean	Only if you're out anyway.
Barbara	Oh yes, don't go specially.

They put coats on etc.

Jean	Lennons' sale previews Thursday.
Barbara	You could gen up on the reductions and then vote . . .
Voice Over	That was a partly political broadcast on behalf of Jean and Barbara.
Barbara	*(Voice Over)* Oh call me Ba, everyone else does!

Continuity

Susie   *(behind her is a map of Britain with flashing lights)* And
Employment Update. Job losses – three thousand in
Paisley and eight hundred in Sunderland with the closure
of GK Metalworks. Job gains – good news in Hove is that
Mrs Mason of the Sea Breeze Restaurant is taking on
somebody to peel the potatoes.

Mr Right

Film. A tidy dull suburban street of semis and front gardens. A small neat woman, Pam, with a shopping trolley, waving to an occasional front window as she passes. She lets herself into one of the houses.

Pam   *(Voice Over)* I believe there's one man in this world that's meant for me, and I'm looking for him quite assiduously, and I'd really quite like him not to be Mexican, just because of the sombrero, it would give us all sorts of problems with the serving-hatch.

The hall of Pam's house, as she takes off her coat, calls hello to her mother, and takes the shopping trolley into the kitchen.

Pam   *(Voice Over)* I've got everything else, suede coat, two-speed hammer drill, and all I need now is Mr Right.

TITLE 'MR RIGHT'

Pam's kitchen. Pam is at the kitchen table, apparently peeling potatoes.

Corin   *(Voice Over)* Pamela Twill is forty-seven. She's never been married, she's never been engaged, she's never been to a Spinners concert with anyone called Roger.

Corin   *(In camera. To Pam)* Has anyone ever proposed, Pam?

Pam   Oh yes, lots of people. A lot of widowers, a deckchair attendant, an anaesthetist, someone who made lampshades out of thermal underwear . . .

Corin   But you've never said yes.

Pam   I've never said yes. I'm looking for Mr Right, Corin. I've met Mr Wrong, I've met several Mr Reasonably OKs, and I've spent a very long afternoon in a bus shelter with Mr Halitosis but –

Corin   Do you think you're too choosy, pernickety?

Pam   No.

Corin   What are you doing with those potatoes?

Pam   Well, before I put them on to boil, I'm just carving them into the faces of minor celebrities, Corin. I've done Cliff Michelmore, here, and Anona Wynn, and I'm just having a crack at Jeremy Beadle.

Corin   And do you do this every time you have boiled potatoes?

Pam   Oh yes, though I wouldn't normally do Jeremy Beadle, because of his perm, but –

Pam's lounge. Pam and her mother, an over-made-up drunken, chainsmoking old tart in a wheelchair. Pam has a coffee, mother has all the makings for a gin and tonic on the tray of her chair.

Mother   You'll never get a man dressed like that anyway, Pam.

Pam   I don't want a man dressed like this. *(Winks at Corin.)*

Mother   When I was your age I wore my blouses so tight my bosoms applied for a transfer. Any more gin?

Pam   In the pantry.

Mother wheels menacingly towards the camera.

Mother   Get out of my bloody way!

Corin   Has your mother always been in a wheelchair?

Pam   Oh, no. She was a very active nymphomaniac for many years, and eventually of course, something snapped . . .

Corin   Is that partly why you've never married – you feel you can't leave her?

Pam   I can't stick her, never mind leave her. No, I'm only – she's still quite insatiable, even now. I mean it's not nice, is it, someone kerb-crawling in an invalid car?

Mother   *(Off)* Well, whereabouts, you sexless dodo?

Pam   Next to the weedkiller! *(Winks at Corin.)* Some hopes!

Pam's office. Three desks. Pam, Margaret and Poll. All very similar, hanging up coats, gloves etc., putting on office cardi's and settling down at their desks.

Pam	*(Voice Over)* I share an office with Margaret and Poll. We dovetail pretty neatly together in the frantic hustle of a typical high-pressure, big-business situation.
Poll	*(reading from newspaper)* Right. Pam – Aquarius. This is a good day for buying a beige headscarf, but make sure it goes into the tumble dryer because you have been caught like that before. Margaret – Aries – your haemorrhoids should be on the wane . . .

Fade out Poll, fade up Corin.

Corin	*(Voice Over)* But today brings a break for Pam from office routine, for, in her ceaseless search for the man of her dreams, she has made an appointment with a computer dating agency.
Poll	*(still reading)* and be particularly wary of salesmen offering low-priced tweezers and denture tablets. Right . . .

Dating agency. Walls covered in wedding photos. Dim girl nervously feeding Pam's details into a computer.

Girl	So what is it – meeting a man with a view to marriage?
Pam	Yes.
Girl	Some of our ladies just want someone to repoint the brickwork. Any particular colour of man?
Pam	No, I don't think so. I'm not nuts on freckles.
Girl	No freckles. What type of personality?
Pam	What type have you?
Girl	Outgoing, homeloving, miserable. You'll find there's quite a big choice at the miserable end of the market.
Pam	Dull, I think. Dull-ish.
Girl	Does he have to be able to –
Pam	Sorry?
Girl	Oosiswhat inter-thingy. Do you wish the marriage to be constipated?
Pam	I –
Girl	Are you looking for physical fill-fullment?
Pam	Yes.
Girl	It's just that some of our gentlemen can't manage that type of activity. They tend to be the miserable ones . . . It's now

searching, and with any luck should come up with the name of your computer date just about now. Ooh, I'm new – it's flashing a recipe for flaky pastry. Mrs Lomax!

Town hall clock (or similar landmark). Pam waiting in her best clothes.

Corin *(Voice Over)* Pam is waiting for her first glimpse of her computer date, Donald Renshaw.

Donald, a perfectly normal-looking fifty-ish businessman, approaches Pam, shakes hands and leads her away.

Corin *(Voice Over)* On paper he's perfect; will Mr Renshaw turn out to be Mr Right?

Restaurant. Pam and Donald being seated at a table. Waiter pulls out Pam's chair as she is sitting down, she falls under the table. He helps her up and gives them both a menu.

Donald Soup of the day, please.
Waiter Yes sir, which one?
Donald Thursday.
Pam *(pointing to item on menu)* Sorry, what are these?
Waiter Grilled mushrooms with garlic, white wine and chopped parsley.
Pam Do you think I could have them without the garlic?
Waiter No garlic.
Pam And no white wine.
Waiter No wine.
Pam And I won't have the mushrooms.
Waiter How would you like the parsley?
Pam Just how it comes, thank you *(waiter leaves)*, but not too chopped.

Time lapse.

Corin *(Voice Over)* Half-way through the main course. How are they getting on?

Pam	No, I think you're right. I think that tablecloth is a slightly different colour.
Donald	Slightly more of an off-white.
Pam	That's right. Sort of white with a hint of beige, as they say.

They fall silent.

Time lapse.

Corin	*(Voice Over)* We're nearing the end of the pudding; has romance flourished over the meringue glacé?
Pam	I think one just has this idea, doesn't one, that in a restaurant like this, all the tablecloths will be the same colour, but –
Donald	It's remarkable how many shades of tablecloth there are just in this one room.
Pam	One room – I agree. As I say – but – er . . .

They fall silent.

Ladies' powder-room. Pam enters, and immediately backs away.

Pam	Oh I'm sorry, I – oh, we're filming.
Corin	Well, to me, Donald seems dull, obsessive, repetitive, humourless and crass. Would you agree?
Pam	Oh definitely – I'm hooked – that's my man!

Doctor's waiting room. Pam sits reading Brides *Magazine.*

Corin	*(Voice Over)* With Pam's marriage to Donald only a week away, she feels the time is right for a little chat with the doctor.

The surgery door opens. A man is ushered out by the doctor, frothing at the mouth, bouncing against the walls like a mad moth etc.

Doctor	As I say, Jim, some people do get a very slight reaction with that one – enjoy your holiday anyway. Miss Twill?

Pam steps over the man who is now staggering to the door on all fours.

Surgery.

Pam	– so I just wanted a little chat before the wedding night, Doctor.
Doctor	Very sensible. What about?
Pam	Well, I've never had physical fill-fullment, and I thought I'd just pop in and get the gen, Doctor.
Doctor	Very wise. Well it's quite simple. The woman has an egg in her waterworks, and this comes to an arrangement with the man's plumbing, and Bob's your uncle. *(Standing up)* Any problems, just pop back and see me.
Pam	Thank you, Doctor.

Pam's back garden. Through the window we can see Donald and mother. Pam and Colin in deckchairs.

Corin	*(Voice Over)* And the final obstacle. Will Pam's mother and Donald get on, or will she turn against him and ban next Thursday's wedding?
Corin	They seem to be getting on quite well.
Pam	Mmmm.
Corin	How do you envisage married life?
Pam	Rather like single, I suppose. I think in my mind's eye I can see a bigger teapot.
Corin	And the intimate side of things?
Pam	Well, I must admit it'll be the first time I've seen a man's pyjama case.

A burst of laughter from inside the house. Ripping noise from Corin's deckchair and he sinks half-way through it. Pam looks at him.

Church. Corin waiting on the steps.

Corin	*(to camera)* Well, it's the big day. Pam asked us not to film the ceremony itself, and with a sensitivity rare amongst documentary film-makers, we've agreed.

Organ music heard from church.

Here they come! Any minute now we'll get our first glimpse
of Mr and Mrs Donald Renshaw.

*Donald comes out of the church pushing mother in her chair, in a
mad wedding dress. Pam, in a neat suit, throws confetti over them.*

Corin   Sorry – Donald – you haven't married Pam's mother?
Mother   Yes, he bloody has! He knows a bit of a swinger when he sees
one. Now put your foot down and get me to the bubbly!

Donald wheels mother away. Pam sweeps up the confetti.

Corin   Pam – this is awful – how do you feel?
Pam   Little bit disappointed, obviously.
Corin   Don't you feel bitter?
Pam   Not really.
Corin   To be their bridesmaid, so generous, and to throw
confetti . . .
Pam   It's poisoned.
Corin   Sorry?
Pam   The confetti. They won't get far.

Pam winks at Corin.

He Didn't: Two

Kelly	So I get to work, right – and I'm just sitting on t'photocopier having a crack at my earwax and in walks Mr Fisher.
Pal	He didn't.
Kelly	He did. Right grumpy. Reeking of Rennies. He says Kelly-Marie Tunstall do you know what time it is? I said yeah I do ta very much.
Pal	You didn't.
Kelly	I did. So he gets right mad and he starts shaking, I love it

	when he does that 'cos all his dandruff drops into his top pocket. He said it's ten-fifteen and I want an explanation. I said all right five minutes ago it was ten past ten, that do yer?
Pal	You didn't.
Kelly	I did. He said I'm waiting, so I parked my chewy on my bra strap and I said – well – I was just posting this coupon for me mam, right – competition – I drink toilet cleaner because . . . okey dokey and this right rabid dog came bounding across the road and bit me right in the pedal-pushers.
Pal	It didn't.
Kelly	It did. So there's somewhat of a commotion, right, and this man came up and he said you know what you've got I said what he said hydrophobia, I said that's that morbid fear of a Cross Channel Ferry and he laughed. Like this. I could see his uvula.
Pal	You couldn't.
Kelly	I could. It were just like the adverts. And he said hydrophobia means you can never ever imbibe water – I said I'm not bothered I only drink Pony – he said no it's right incredibly dangerous and you have to have an operation right now!
Pal	He didn't.
Kelly	He did. And he said and fortunately I'm qualified to do it, though I'm actually a tree surgeon and I've only ever done it on a sycamore. Well, he hadn't got any anaesthetic so I had a right big whiff of *Rive Gauche* and next thing I knew I was on the ten o'clock bus completely cured.
Pal	You weren't.
Kelly	I was. But Mr Fisher's gone a bit puce, right. I said you want to study the heart disease statistics in the British Medical Journal, you do. He said Kelly-Marie Tunstall you have been repeatedly warned for persistent lateness and coming to work in a nightie, I've a good mind to fire you on the spot.
Pal	He didn't.
Kelly	He did. I said you can fire away, but I'm not leaving otherwise I'll tell everyone what happened on Christmas Eve when you drank two pints of correcting fluid and sexually harassed me with an outsize party squeaker.
Pal	He didn't.
Kelly	No he didn't – he nibbled my Twiglets and passed out – but it shut him up.

We're Half Asleep

Logo and signature tune 'We're Half Asleep!'. Bleak little studio. Girl presenter, fiddling with her hair, realizes she's on air but isn't too bothered.

Girl   Oh, right. OK. Well, a lot of you have been to zoos I suppose, and seen a lot of ezotic, sorry, exoktic, God I can't talk this morning, exotic animals. Right? But have you ever thought of keeping one in your back garden? Well, someone who has, or does rather, has thought of it, does do it, whatever, is er Louise erm Louise, God I've been getting this name wrong all morning – Louise Kazinski.

She strolls over to po-faced thirteen-year-old.

Hello, Louise.
Louise   Hello.
Girl   It is Kazinski – I got that right, didn't I?
Louise   Not really.
Girl   So, what have you brought along to show us?
Louise   What?
Girl   Weren't you bringing something, or something?
Louise   No, you can't travel them about really.
Girl   What's that?
Louise   Alligators.
Girl   Oh right, got you. Alligators. Dummee. No, you see *(to camera)* someone had scribbled over my running-order thing and there was a word beginning with 'a' and I thought it said animals but it said alligators so there we go. Right, Louise, alligators – how many have you got?
Louise   Ten, at the moment.
Girl   Ten, gosh, it must be quite a problem finding room for them all, what do you do, keep them in the bath?
Louise   No, we've built an artificial environment –

Girl	Really, gosh, that must be quite difficult. And how many have you got?
Louise	Ten – I –
Girl	Gosh, that's quite a lot. And are they little tiny ones, they're presumably not the great big ones?
Louise	Well, up to five feet long.
Girl	Gosh, that's quite big. They must take up quite a lot of space, where on earth do you keep them all?
Louise	My father's built a kind of art –
Girl	Dad's sorted something out has he, that's good. Fathers do have their uses, though not if they glug away at the old gin bottle like mine does, anyway, shouldn't have said that really, never mind, er – right, so – how big actually are they, actually?
Louise	Well, in the wild they can grow up to ten feet, but they don't grow that much in captivity.
Girl	Ten feet, gosh, that's quite a lot of feet isn't it, and how many have you got of those?
Louise	Well, ten, but like I said – our ones –
Girl	*(interrupting)* Yes, well, ten times ten, says she doing her maths bit, one hundred feet, just about isn't it, quite a lot of crocodile.
Louise	Yes.
Girl	Really? Well, thanks very much for coming along Louise – I'm sure we've all learnt a lot of new things we didn't already know. One thing I must ask you – how many alligators have you actually got?
Louise	Ten.
Girl	Gosh, as many as that.

Lights fade but not sound.

Right, that's it – we just have to look as if we're talking now, it just makes a better picture. So where do you find room for them all anyway, in the bath?

The Trolley

Restaurant – lunchtime – businessmen. Two completely straight businessmen, waiting for pudding.

Alan   Well, those figures sound very promising, Tim – how's Plymouth looking?

Tim   *(waggling hand)* Plymouth? Either way, Alan, either way – it's on hold – I feel personally Plymouth could be another Exeter.

Alan   Really? That's interesting.

Tim   We're very much keeping an ear to the ground with Plymouth.

Alan   I think what the regional boys tend to forget –

He breaks off as extremely dim waitress arrives with sweet trolley.

             Tim?

Tim   Alan?

Alan   Just coffee thank you – yeah, the regional boys –

Tim   Yes, just coffee for me too please – regional boys?

Alan   Is that we have to consider the Isle of Wight as well.

They notice the waitress is still there with the trolley.

             Two coffees, yes?

Waitress Coffees what?

Alan   What?

Waitress Have you seen it?

Alan   *(completely lost but trying not to lose face)* Erm –

Waitress Have you seen it on the trolley?

Alan   Just two coffees, no sweet.

Waitress Just two coffees no sweet?

Alan   That's it. What was I – the Isle of Wight –

Waitress	Have you seen it on the trolley?
Alan	*(no idea what she's talking about)* No, yes, thank you.
Waitress	Is it a sorbet?
Alan	Just the coffees, thank you. Now, er, Plymouth –
Waitress	Can you point at it?
Alan	No, we don't want anything on the trolley.
Waitress	Oh, anything on the trolley.
Alan	No, just take the trolley away dear, thank you, and we'll just have coffee, thank you.

She wheels it away.

Tim	*(to cover a sticky moment)* I must give you the print-out from Expo – it came out pretty much as you predicted –

The waitress wheels the trolley back.

Alan	Yes, so I believe . . .
Waitress	They're good castors, aren't they? I been right over to cutlery.
Alan	We don't want a pudding, we have a lot to discuss –
Waitress	You don't want a pudding.
Alan	Right.
Waitress	But you're having a sweet.
Tim	Er love – we're just having the old 'café', coffee.
Alan	I'll handle this Tim, thanks very much.
Waitress	Coffee.
Alan	Coffee.
Waitress	Is it on the trolley?
Alan	I asked you to take the trolley away.
Waitress	I did do.
Alan	Then you brought it back.
Waitress	Then I brought it back.
Alan	Now – take it away –
Waitress	Take it away what?
Alan	The trolley.
Waitress	The trolley. Take it away, the trolley.
Alan	And don't bring it back.
Waitress	What? The trolley!

She wheels it away

Tim	That sorted that out anyway, Alan.
Alan	Yes, well, just don't butt in next time OK, promotion's not automatic, you know.

Pause.

	Yes, there, er, Expo figures – Colin phoned them through to the top floor –
Tim	Now I didn't know that.
Alan	Oh yes, that's fairly automatic since the shake-up –

She wheels it back in.

Waitress	What did you say after take the trolley away?
Alan	Get me the bill.
Waitress	Get me the bill. No, it wasn't that.
Alan	I want the bill.
Waitress	Can you point at it?
Alan	Listen to me.

The Waitress listens intently.

	Are you listening to me?
Waitress	I was just then – have I to carry on?
Alan	I am not going to stand up and make a scene. Please fetch, to this table, now, the headwaiter, the man in the dark jacket pouring the wine. Just bring him here, please.
Waitress	Can you mind my trolley?
Alan	Yes.

She goes. They sit in tense silence. The head waiter arrives, suave Italian.

Head waiter	Is everything all right for you, sir? I trust the meal was to your liking, and how can I be of assistance?
Alan	I would like the bloody bill, please.
Head waiter	The bloody bill. *(In waitress's voice, with her expression)* Is it on the trolley?

He didn't: Three

Kelly   Anyway, so. I'm stretched out in my new swimming costume, right – cut up here, cut down here, keyhole *(indicating leg, chest and midriff)* and I'm boiling hot and the light's burning my eyes and my mam comes up and says Kelly-Marie Tunstall will you switch that cooker off and get off that ironing board.

Pal   She didn't.

Kelly	She did. And we're having our tea, right, pommes lyonnaise and spam nuggets – and she said you'd better know – I'm running away with a nuclear physicist and if you look behind the clock you'll find fifteen quid and a bag of oven chips.
Pal	She didn't.
Kelly	She did. She said when your dad comes in tell him not to try and find me 'cos I'm changing my name, cutting my hair and laughing on the other side of my face.
Pal	She didn't.
Kelly	She did. And she laughed. Like this. I said I hope that's not hereditary 'cos it hurts your eyeballs. She said well actually you're adopted – you were left on my doorstep wrapped in the business section of the *Sunday Times*.
Pal	You weren't.
Kelly	I was. And it's right embarrassing when you're fourteen. She said your real father is a right prominent rhythm guitarist and your mother does the ironing for University Challenge.
Pal	She doesn't.
Kelly	She does. Then I got this letter, right, all typed – loads of spelling – it said Kelly-Marie Tunstall your father has been killed whilst falling under a bus, and you might be in for one million pounds and half-shares in a stationary caravan at Cleveleys.
Pal	It didn't.
Kelly	It did. So I went to see the solicitor, right, all dressed up – black bondage outfit, tan accessories, and he said Kelly-Marie Tunstall, I'm going to give you a cheque for one million pounds, and all you have to do is give up Babycham, learn the oboe, and have one thigh tattoed with a crude caricature of Rupert Murdoch.
Pal	He didn't.
Kelly	He did! *(Shows tattoed thigh.)* So I had that done, learnt the oboe and then I phoned up and told him to stuff it. What's the point of having a million pounds if you can't get legless on Babycham? Eh?

Lady Police Serial

Juliet and Wilberforce, the desk sergeant, chatting at the front desk. They both have their hats on.

Juliet	Wilberforce.
Wilberforce	Ma'am?
Juliet	Do you mind if I ask you something?
Wilberforce	I don't, no.
Juliet	Do you know how to make a cup of tea?
Wilberforce	No, I don't, ma'am.
Juliet	No, neither do I. *(Bangs on desk.)* And I should know! Wilberforce – I've just had a call from Harry Potter.
Wilberforce	Harry Potter the safebreaker? Little feller? Black 'tache, hangs round The Mop and Bucket, easily led but unexpectedly generous?
Juliet	That's him. Do you know him?
Wilberforce	No. What did he want, ma'am?
Juliet	I don't know, we were cut off before he could tell me. He might have been murdered – I'll pop round on my way home. What happened about the brick that went missing from the building site, Wilberforce?
Wilberforce	It's been found, ma'am. It's chipped along one corner, but they think it's going to be all right.
Juliet	That's good. Our Asian friends – are they still being racially harrassed?
Wilberforce	No. Those National Front skinheads have completely changed their tune, thanks to you. In fact, they're throwing a party for the entire Asian community tomorrow.
Juliet	Right. I thought that new ping-pong table would do the trick. I might go to the party, Wilberforce – I've got a serge sari – where is it being held?
Wilberforce	Kitchener Street, ma'am – five streets away from the old playground where someone who did some shoplifting's

mother was found wandering in a confused state – do you know it?

Juliet Yes, I do. It backs on to the Cut where old Barney the tramp drowned himself because his dog had been run over by a Bedford van – I forget the registration number.

Wilberforce We all had a whip-round, ma'am, as you suggested, and bought him a new puppy.

Juliet Did it work?

Wilberforce Yes, the old tramp's alive again now. In fact, he's thinking of doing social sciences at the Open University.

Message comes through on the radio.

Voice Oscar Delta Tango Charlie Farnsbarns to base, over.

Juliet grabs the mike.

Juliet I'll deal with this, Wilberforce. You go and check on Garstang's Television and Video Rental shop in the High

Street. I passed there this morning and some of those televisions looked like they were about to be stolen.

Wilberforce Right away, ma'am. *(Leaves.)* I've just got to get some after-dinner mints and change my library books.

Juliet Good lad.

Wilberforce *(stopping in doorway)* Where is the High Street, ma'am?

Juliet Not sure, Wilberforce. Ask when you get there.

He leaves. She speaks into mike.

Oscar Delta Tango Charlie Farnsbarns, come in please – this is Bippetty Boppetty Eggwhisk Goulash Pantiegirdle, over.

Voice There's an incident taking place on the moors, ma'am.

Juliet Got that. Anything else I should know?

Voice It's quite windy.

Juliet Will I need a poncho?

Voice You might need a sheepskin coat.

Juliet I'm on my way. Don't do anything stupid, Constable.

Voice   Like what, ma'am?
Juliet   Hot air ballooning. It can be very dangerous given bad
             weather conditions like those you've described. I'll be
             with you as soon as I've had a good cry, because I'm only
             a woman and from time to time the pressure gets to me,
             tough as I am. Over and out. Wah!

Self-service

Department store, upmarket self-service counter. Extremely long slow queue. A couple of girls serving behind. Our two nice ladies are at the end of the queue by the trays. Enid has a beret and no hair visible.

Enid	*(taking a tray)* Do you know, I've scoured this store from top to bottom, can I find a side-winding thermal body belt, can I buffalo.
Wyn	What did you want one for?
Enid	*(handing her tray over the counter)* Excuse me – I think you'll find there's spam on that. *(Taking another tray)* That gippy kidney.
Wyn	Flared up?
Enid	I'll say – it's like being continually poked – can you imagine that? *(Wyn can't.)* Dr Brewster says if I don't keep it lagged for the winter I could be spending a penny every twenty minutes come March.
Wyn	Can't they operate?
Enid	I haven't time to go in. I'm on the phone day and night about that carpet. What's the soup, dear?
Girl	Country vegetable.
Enid	What country – Taiwan?
Wyn	Have they not sent it? Your carpet. *(Rootles round the counter.)* There's croutons.
Enid	With my molars? Filthy French habit. Oh they sent it – I sent it back. I said, 'Do I look like a woman who would grace her lobby with a bordered Axminster?' I've told them time beyond number I'm the wall-to-wall elephant.
Wyn	Is that steak?
Enid	I would doubt it. Probably some poor beast that came a cropper at Beechers Brook. Er, dear – is this fish boned?
Girl	No.
Enid	I should check your insurance. Then I had a huge to-do

	and hoohah at the hairdressers.
Wyn	What about these Dublin prawns?
Enid	Never touch prawns. Do you know, they hang round sewage outlet pipes treading water with their mouths open – they love it!
Wyn	Still going to Maison Renée?
Enid	Chez Maurice was putting out feelers . . .
Wyn	Oh no, he reeks of neutralizer.
Enid	And he's forever dabbing at his cold sores with *Old Spice* –
Wyn	Aren't prawns an aphrodisiac?
Enid	I wouldn't put it past them. Well, I'm at Renée's – waiting to be shampooed – flicking through a *Woman's Weekly* – lovely piece on Alma Cogan. *(They've now reached veg, and the queue's stopped.)* Sorry – what's the hold-up here, dear?
Girl	We're waiting for fresh cauli . . .
Enid	Fresh! You might as well wait for Maurice Chevalier. So I'm called into the cubicle – it's all separate at Renée's – not like these terrible modern places where you find yourself sharing a perm trolley with two footballers – *(annoyed at the delay)* this is ridiculous *(pushing past the veg waiters)*. Can I thrust by – I'm a diabetic.

They are now at the sweet section.

	So in comes Renée.
Wyn	She must be getting on.
Enid	Well, this is the trouble. If she leans too far forward with a sponge roller she topples out of her walking frame – and you really have to shout up – I don't particularly want the whole world knowing I'm not a natural conker.
Wyn	Is that trifle?
Enid	It may have been in a previous existence. *(Elaborately casually looking away)* Don't have the gateaux – I just saw her scratching her armpit with the cake slice. And Renée's very set in her ways, style-wise – I don't mind – I'm a great admirer of Phyllis Calvert.
Wyn	So why hence the hoohah?
Enid	Well, I decided to go a shade mad because we've the Smoked Meat Purveyors Buffet 'n' Mingle at the weekend.

Irate voice from a woman a couple of people further down the queue.

Woman   Could we get by please; we're not having a sweet.

Woman and friend push by our two.

Enid   Very wise, with those hips. So I said, 'Skip the conker, Renée – I'll have burnished beech-nut and to heck with it.'
Wyn   So?
Enid   Well, you know she's colour blind and they've only a gas mantle round the back?
Wyn   Colour blind?
Enid   Can't tell red from blue. Once tottered into a brothel thinking it was a police station.

They reach Tea, Coffee and the Till.

Second girl Tea, Coffee?
Enid   No.
Wyn   She didn't.
Enid   Oh, it was all right – one of the girls came out and helped her pump her tyres up.
Second girl Sorry, are you still waiting for something?
Enid   Yes, a small mineral water and an orange squash, please.
Second girl Water and squash back down the end by the trays. *(To next customer)* Tea, Coffee?

Enid and Wyn leave their trays behind and push past everybody back to the starting point. They pick up two trays and rejoin the queue.

Enid   You've a look of Eva Braun, did you know? Well – what Renée mixed up in the back – burnished beech-nut it was not – more like varicose violet – I could have wept.

Engrossed, they move off again – past the water and squash – people behind them as before.

Wyn	Did you have to pay?
Enid	Well, she knocked off my bourbons but – *(they move along)*. Then in comes Maxine, waving her whitlow . . .
Wyn	Is she the bodybuilder?
Enid	No that's Lois *(start to fade)*. No, Maxine's the one I told you about – excuse me – grey eggs – is that an Arab custom?

Cast List

All the sketches in this volume were first performed in *Victoria Wood As Seen on TV* (2nd series), shown on BBC2 in November, 1986, with the exception of the first six episodes of 'Acorn Antiques', which were performed in the first series, shown on BBC2 in January, 1985, and those marked with a *, first performed in a special programme on BBC television in autumn 1987.

Nora	*Nora*	Victoria Wood
No Gossip	*1st Lady*	Victoria Wood
	2nd Lady	Julie Walters
Margery and Joan	*Margery*	Julie Walters
	Joan	Victoria Wood
Men Talking	*1st Man*	Michael Nightingale
	2nd Man	Eric Richards
	3rd Man	Graham Seed
Today in Hospital	*Corin*	Duncan Preston
	Cleaner	Peter Martin
	Receptionist	Heather Baskerville
	Elaine	Victoria Wood
	Conrad	Andrew Livingston
	Doctor	Benjamin Whitrow
	Mrs Jones	Myrtle Devonish
	1st Student	Nicholas Barnes
	2nd Student	Ravindar Valia
	3rd Student	Richard Brenner
	Noreen	Kathryn Apanowicz
	Della	Beverly Martin
	Kevin	Philip Lowrie
	Drunken Man	Clive Panto
Kitty	*Kitty*	Patricia Routledge
Salesman	*Man*	Duncan Preston
	Woman	Celia Imrie
Reports Local	*Man*	Duncan Preston

	Woman	Celia Imrie
Dr Who*	*Doctor*	Jim Broadbent
	Fiona	Georgia Allen
	Crayola	Duncan Preston
	Guard	Johnny Worthy
Craft Shop	*Owner*	Rosalind March
	Girl	Celia Imrie
Wine Bar	*Man*	Ronnie Letham
	Girl	Carolyn Pickles
Acorn Antiques	*Babs*	Celia Imrie
	Mrs Overall	Julie Walters
	Clifford	Duncan Preston
	Bertha	Victoria Wood
	Trixie	Rosie Collins
	Derek	Kenny Ireland
	Jerez	Peter Ellis
	Extras	Albert & Michaela Welch
The Making of	*Marion Clune*	Maggie Steed
Acorn Antiques*	*Simon*	Sam Kelly
	Roberts	Nicholas Barnes
	Mickey	Bryan Burdon
	Make-up Girl	Jane Hardy
	PA	Deborah Grant
	Assistant Floor Manager	Colin Simmonds
Spaghetti	*Philippa*	Julie Walters
	Faith	Victoria Wood
	Waiter	Gerard Kelly
Medical School	*1st Man*	Terence Longdon
	2nd Man	Duncan Preston
	Sarah	Victoria Wood
	Woman	Celia Imrie
He Didn't	*Kelly*	Victoria Wood
	Pal	Mary Jo Randle
Tattoo Parlour	*Woman*	Victoria Wood
	Eric	Michael Gunn
	Paul	Gerard Kelly
Partly Political Broadcast	*Barbara*	Julie Walters
	Jean	Victoria Wood
Susie (Continuity)*	*Susie*	Susie Blake

Mr Right	*Pam*	Anne Reid
	Corin	Duncan Preston
	Mother	Dora Bryan
	Poll	Meg Johnson
	Girl	Victoria Wood
	Donald	Michael Nightingale
	Waiter	David Adams
	Doctor	John Nettleton
We're Half Asleep	*Girl*	Celia Imrie
	Louise	Nadine Wilson
The Trolley	*Alan*	Graham Seed
	Tim	Duncan Preston
	Waitress	Victoria Wood
	Head Waiter	Chris Sanders
Lady Police Serial	*Juliet*	Victoria Wood
	Wilberforce	Duncan Preston
	Voice	Stephen Hancock
Self-service*	*Enid*	Julie Walters
	Wyn	Victoria Wood
	1st Girl	Sue Wallace
	Woman	Celia Imrie
	2nd Girl	Lill Roughley